A Rebel's Guide to a
Why-Centered Lifestyle

Destiny Burns

REBEL QUEEN OF REINVENTION

NEWMAN SPRINGS PUBLISHING
320 Broad Street
Red Bank, NJ 07701

First originally published by Newman Springs Publishing 2023

Cover and interior design by Fran Greelis, Frantic Productions, Inc.
Edited by Gail Kerzner, The Savvy Red Pen
Photo credits: Alana Kirk Photography and Destiny Burns

ISBN 979-8-88763-785-3 (Paperback)
ISBN 979-8-88763-786-0 (Digital)

Library of Congress Control Number: 2023901211

Printed in the United States of America

The two most important days in your life are the day you are born and the day you find out why.

—Mark Twain

MY WHY AND I
DEDICATION
AND ACKNOWLEDGMENTS

...

I dedicate this book to my Aimee. Not only is she my daughter, but she's also my beloved friend, my infinite inspiration, and my greatest joy. She came right through me into this world, and I'm profoundly grateful to be her mama. Since the moment I found out I was pregnant with her, her well-being has been at the essence of my *why*. I consider it my greatest responsibility to encourage her to be true to herself and provide her with an environment of unconditional love and support. It continues to be an incredible privilege to watch her discover, learn, and grow into the amazing woman she has become. I've always tried to live my life in a way that would be a positive example to her, and I see shades of myself and my influence in her character. What truly makes me beam with pride is seeing her embrace and live her own *why* and witness the incredible impact she's making in our world as a result. I'm so in awe of the inspiration she has given me through her example and her courage, creativity, kindness, and wisdom. There are simply no words to express how much I love her. Thanks, Aims.

I also want to convey immense love and gratitude for my wonderful family and the many friends, mentors, colleagues, and supporters who have been instrumental in encouraging me to live my *why* throughout my life. I never could have soared without the safety net of your support, encouragement, and guidance. Thank you so much!

MY WHY AND I

CONTENTS

FOREWORD

BY KERRY HANNON

. . .

We are so fortunate when we cross paths with someone who simply inspires us. It might be their moxie, their intellect, or the way they view the possibilities of life and reach for them with all their heart.

Well, that's Destiny Burns.

I first met Destiny when I was eager to learn from midlife entrepreneurial women who had tackled major career transitions to start a second act. Her journey so motivated me that I knew I had to share it far and wide. You'll see why when you weave your way through her instructive and enlightening new book, *My Why and I*.

She's a rebel. She has that spark about her. But she's a rebel with a plan and an inner core of confidence. She understands reinvention is in many ways a redeployment of the skills and qualities you already have deep inside you kindled by new learning and curiosity. "Not all reinventions are earth-shattering upheavals where everything needs to change (although some are)," she writes. "They are all deliberate, however. Many reinventions are tweaks or adjustments to your attitude, approach, and execution of the way you're living your life, investing your energy, and spending your time and effort."

Destiny openly shares her path with you in this book. She explains her *why* that has helped her chart her course for decades, and then she helps you discover your own.

She's a trusted guide who has walked the walk. She knows how it feels to make significant life transitions and do the necessary work involved, including the deep inner exploration that is never easy but essential to lay the stable groundwork to succeed.

Entrepreneurs like Destiny and, hopefully, you—whether you're building a business or embarking on rebuilding your life in a new direction—concentrate on what you want to craft and build rather than on the stumbling blocks. As my father always told me, "You have to dream to get there."

Destiny dug in and faced her challenges squarely and steadily. "Fear is a reinvention motivation killer," she writes. "Fear keeps you stuck and saps your will."

She's boldly honest. She admits, "As I navigated every single one of my own reinventions, there were so many times when I was completely terrified! I was often afraid to let go of the life I knew, even if it was no longer serving me. I was terrified of failure."

In the new world of work, entrepreneurship will be a go-to solution for a growing number of adults over fifty who have either a burning desire to be their own boss or have grown disenchanted and discouraged by the job hunt and yearn to take control of their purpose.

When Destiny headed to her childhood hometown in Cleveland, Ohio, to create CLE Urban Winery (a winery and tasting room in a 5,000-square-foot garage), it seemed like a bit of an unlikely next act for her. She had enjoyed a twenty-year military career with posts around the world from Japan to the Persian Gulf. After she retired from active duty in 2003, she spent thirteen years in business development positions for defense contractors such as General Dynamics and Northrop Grumman. But she was restless.

A series of major life events shifted her mindset and gave her the impetus to step it up. "I had always dreamed of having my own business," she told me. "I had a desire to do something different and to, well, feed my soul. No matter where I lived around the world, Cleveland was my home. It represented family and a place where I had always found happiness."

Once Destiny made the decision to go home again, she began her inner journey to explore that MRI of her soul: to identify what she had loved in her life and the times that brought a smile and satisfaction, a sense of well-being.

And that's precisely what she'll guide you to do.

Big changes don't happen overnight. Destiny spent roughly two years doing her groundwork before she launched her business.

Many entrepreneurs at this stage of life are spurred into action after experiencing a life crisis or major personal shift of some kind. Perhaps it's a health issue, divorce (as Destiny experienced), or someone close to them dying at a young age.

And each person has a flexible time horizon for their venture. You might know you want to do something new but don't have the nerve to do it yet. Take a breath.

"You have to trust yourself," Destiny told me. "For me, it was extremely hard to leave a steady job and the money behind. But once I knew what I wanted to do and decided I could do it, I drew the line in the sand and kept going forward. One key for me was to do at least one thing every day to move the concept forward until it became a reality. Sometimes all that meant was making a phone call or completing some market research, but it helped me crystallize what I was doing. It kept it real."

Destiny understands the reality of making dramatic changes in one's life and the positive impact it has not only on you but also on the world around you.

That's what rebels do. In this book, you'll find a clear-eyed vision of how to navigate your future through exploration and give yourself permission to be open to unexpected invitations without that lingering fear.

Rebels like Destiny—and you—take control of their lives by heading down new trails, following dreams, and embracing a future of possibility and joy. And that's a rebellious path worth taking.

Kerry Hannon is a workplace futurist and strategist on career transitions, entrepreneurship, personal finance, and retirement. She is a frequent TV, radio, and podcast commentator and is a sought-after keynote speaker. She is currently a senior columnist for Yahoo Finance and an on-air expert. She was formerly an expert columnist, opinion writer, and regular contributor to *The New York Times*, MarketWatch, and *Forbes* and a personal finance and entrepreneurship expert on the PBS website NextAvenue.org. She has appeared as a career and financial expert on *Dr. Phil*, ABC, CBS, CNBC, *NBC Nightly News*, NPR, Yahoo Finance, and PBS. Kerry has dedicated her work to making a difference in people's lives, to give them confidence and the tools to succeed personally, professionally, and financially. She offers her audiences and readers can-do expert advice on the best ways to empower themselves now and for the future.

MY WHY AND I
PREFACE

...

Conventional wisdom says that you only live once. Why would we ever want to confine ourselves to that premise? My rebellious and revolutionary theory is that although we all have one life to live, we can and should live many different lives of purpose within that one lifetime. The scope, quality, and impact of our lives are limited only by our imagination and passion—or by our fear.

The concept of "reinvention" is most often used when we find ourselves living a life that makes us unhappy, leaves us unfulfilled, or puts us at a crossroad. If we could get a new job, move to a new place, make more money, lose weight, or leave an unsatisfying relationship, our lives would transform. These things are *whats* and, to my unconventional way of thinking, these what-driven changes alone will not fix what's lacking. Lasting transformative reinvention should be driven by *whys*, not by *whats*.

Keeping your why at the center of your life as a beacon of truth and light is a lifestyle choice. It does *not* happen by accident. You must do it on purpose and with purpose to achieve truly life-changing results. To this rebel's way of thinking, committing to living your life continually centered on your why is my definition of real reinvention.

My mission is to make you think about reinvention differently. It isn't a destination—it's a movement! My vision of reinvention is a revolutionary design for living. This approach isn't "one and done" or just having a "second act." Instead, I want to create a worldwide mindset shift that comes with adopting the rebellious philosophy that reinvention is a continuum.

Our *why* should drive our lives, and it changes and evolves all the time as we learn and grow throughout our life. Listening to your why is a skill that requires practice to become second nature. I want to share my hard-earned experience about adopting the concept of a why-centered lifestyle: how I did it, why I did it, and what it has meant to the quality and impact of my own life. Let's break the rules and live the life of our dreams!

As I reflected upon my own life's journey, I uncovered the pattern of a reinvention continuum in my life that I've been navigating since I was a teenager. Once I discovered this and the powerful message it conveyed, I felt called to share it with others. This is my *why* I am living today, or at least a part of it (much more on that later). When I looked back on the continuum of my lifetime of reinventions, I saw the patterns and processes I used repeatedly and captured them in this book. It's taken me almost half a century to understand the power of this approach.

My vision of living a why-centered lifestyle is a bit like committing to a vegan way of life. We all eat; we need food to live. At every meal, we make decisions about what we put into our bodies as fuel. Sometimes these choices are based on taste, cost, or convenience—in other words, *whats*. We often eat mindlessly, not giving much thought to our food choices and their impact on our health and well-being. We may go on a diet when we can see and feel that our food choices impact us negatively. It's hard to make dietary changes stick. Building a lifestyle around how we fuel our bodies requires more focus and discipline than a quickly abandoned fad diet.

Committing to a vegan diet means deliberately not eating many foods that others do. The why for doing this may be improved health or living personal or moral beliefs. My point is those who view dietary choices as a lifestyle rather than meal by meal are much more likely to be motivated by the why driving these choices. The resulting lifestyle is more likely to manifest long-term and impactful benefits than a fad diet ever could. A lifestyle choice is a deliberate decision of truth and authenticity, whether it involves the food we put on our plates or how we live our daily lives. Do you want to nourish your soul throughout your life or keep it on a fast-food diet?

The COVID-19 pandemic shook up the world and forced us all to prioritize what's important. It made us reimagine work-life balance, who we are, and why we do things. It revealed new ways of thinking, living, and serving that had previously been unimaginable. So many people previously had their heads down, grinding through daily life because they thought they had no choice. This societal disruption showed us we all have the freedom and opportunity to imagine new possibilities and make different choices. You don't have to accept a life that doesn't fulfill your needs, dreams, and desires. It's up to you, though, to make the delightfully rebellious decision and commitment to doing something about it. You'll need help along the way to reach your new destinations, but the choice to take that first step and live that why-centered lifestyle belongs to you alone. Be your own rebel queen (or king)!

MY WHY AND I

INTRODUCTION

READY FOR A REINVENTION REVOLUTION?

...

I'm a rebel *with* a cause, and my calling is to take you on the journey of a lifetime.

This is not your standard "self-help" book, and it is not for the faint of heart. This book is a passport to a new way of life, centered on living your *why*. A why-centered lifestyle takes focus, reflection, dedication, bravery, and hard work, but the results are transformational. I'll be your guide as you learn to embrace your true self and trust your gut. You'll fight your fear and create your road map, and then you'll leap into new directions and accept new challenges that will make the rebel inside you rejoice.

I hereby and forever claim my crown as the Rebel Queen of Reinvention, and I wear my hard-earned crown with pride! Even if that crown is a little cockeyed and tarnished sometimes, it's still my most prized metaphorical possession. I've been reinventing myself since I was sixteen, and I'll do so as often as necessary to continually live a why-centered lifestyle. Realignment and reinvention on repeat are a way of life for me and are my keys to living a rebellious life of authenticity. It's a gift I've given myself repeatedly over a lifetime. I want you to have this gift in your own life. Let's do this!

As the reigning Rebel Queen of Reinvention, I don't just talk the talk. I also walk the walk. In this book, I offer as examples and inspiration the many and widely varied personal and professional reinventions I've undertaken in my own life to live in alignment with my why. That's what it's all about. That's the goal. This rebel's guidebook will teach you how to reinvent yourself, feed your soul, and make your heart sing. As we take this journey together, I'll show you how to imagine new possibilities and achieve new goals that enable you to continually realign to your why.

This book is part memoir and part practical guide on "Reinvention for Rebels" who want to know *how*—and, most importantly, *why*—to realign with their why and reinvent on an ongoing basis. This guide isn't focused on career change, although a career change may be necessary to achieve the alignment you seek. Instead, this book focuses on life change, building and living a new attitude for how and why you live your life every day.

We shouldn't fear challenges, rejections, setbacks, and wanted or unwanted change. They can be the best things to ever happen to us. These catalysts can reveal opportunities for transformative reinvention of your life in new, exciting, and unexpected directions. You have the ultimate power to determine the life you'll lead, the impact you'll make, and the legacy you'll leave. Reinvention requires focus, passion, calculated risk, and the courage to bet on yourself. You're the ruler of your own life, and no one else has that power or right to rule over you unless you abdicate your throne and surrender your crown. I know I won't be doing that anytime soon!

I'm not the least bit conventional. I never have been. I'm type A-plus and a proverbial bulldozer. I always trust my gut like my life depends on it, but I'm also highly information- and process-driven. My approach to reinvention, which is as unconventional as I am, has worked for me for more than forty years. I don't take the first tactical step toward a new lifestyle goal or ambition before knowing my core values and defining my why first. Once I do that, I know I can confidently move forward and bring my why-centered lifestyle plans to fruition. In this book, I'll walk you through my proven process to do that, complete with all the tools and tips you'll need.

Is it possible to be both a rebel queen and a process geek? Hell yes! I'm living proof. Using the Gestalt method of experience sharing, I use my own rebellious life of repeat reinvention and my related lessons learned and stories as a guide. I show you how these reinventions kept me aligned with my why. I share my best tricks and techniques. I explain my overarching process for repeatable why-centered realignment and reinvention that uses visioning and planning techniques to overcome fear. I help you inventory and leverage existing skills, resources, and experiences so you can identify and fill gaps and explore ways to persevere through setbacks. Last but not least, I discuss how to remain in tune and in relationship with your why as it changes or evolves so you'll know when to repeat this process.

A gift isn't really a gift until you give it to someone else. As I share my gift with you in this book, I hope it speaks to you and benefits you in your journey as much as it benefits mine and as much as I love sharing it. Continually living a life of purpose and inspiration requires us to understand that reinvention is a continuum, not a singular destination. Once we internalize that and let our core values and our why guide us, we can live a life of lasting fulfillment. Ready to be a rebel?

CHAPTER1

1

CLAIM YOUR CROWN AND
LIVE YOUR WHY

...

I'm a rebel *with* a process! In this chapter, I'll provide an overview of the process I've successfully used repeatedly to realign and reinvent myself to manifest my why-centered lifestyle. In subsequent chapters, we'll deep dive into the specific tips, tools, and experience shares for all the steps that will guide you in your reinvention journey so you can claim your own crown as a reinvention rebel.

Your why can also be referred to as passion, motive, conviction, calling, pull, or drive. It serves as the fuel for your reinvention, makes it stick, and channels its purpose. True reinvention—whether the total shake-up variety or a minor soul realignment—can be difficult. It challenges you, but it can also be invigorating and magnificent. It can be uncomfortable and messy, but it can also be exhilarating and fun.

LIVING A WHY-CENTERED LIFESTYLE

To know where you're going, you first must know where you are and, more importantly, why you're there. Do your current situation, environment, and conditions match up with your why and your core values? My process will help you discover the honest answer to that question and provide guidance to take actions that can profoundly change your life. Our lives often pull or push us in directions that don't fulfill us. The rebellious part of this philosophy is the willful act of taking control of your own life to fix that.

This book presents my proven six-step process, which will help you to *realign*, *reinvent*, and *repeat* so you can clarify, commit to, and confirm your why-centered lifestyle. This process is deliberately interlinked. Where you start and where you finish within the process continuum depends on where your why is leading you and what you want or need to accomplish to align with it. Process-driven reinvention may not seem very rebellious, but take it from this type A-plus nerdy rebel—it works.

The six steps associated with these core components serve as stepping stones to move you through the process. You may want to use all the steps, progressing through them sequentially, or you may only need to leverage a few specific steps and tools to get the desired results. It all depends on where you are, what you need, and what outcomes you're looking to achieve. I've designed the process so you can tailor it to your own journey.

The extent of the transformation required to stay aligned with your why depends on many factors. Not all reinventions are earth-shattering upheavals where everything needs to change, although some are! However, they are all deliberate. Many reinventions are tweaks or adjustments to your attitude, approach, and execution of the way you're living your life, investing your energy, and spending your time and effort. The objective is to achieve the resulting change and the alignment that fulfills you.

My process provides the flexibility to meet you where you are. For example, you may already have a strong clarity about your why. You can then dig into the steps of the process to break through your fears, build your dream team, acquire new skills, and create a solid plan to achieve your goals. When you run into roadblocks, my process can also help you persevere and triumph over them to reach your why-centered lifestyle destination. In addition, my process will teach you how to remain continually attuned to your why so you know when it's time to realign and reinvent again.

The first time you go through this, I recommend you start in the Realign portion of the continuum. Moving forward, you may choose to begin your next quest for reinvention in another part of the process because each piece feeds into and on each other.

Living a why-centered lifestyle is iterative; there's no real finish line. We are all works in progress, so it makes sense that our ambition to continually live our why is also going to be a work in progress.

REALIGN: KNOW YOUR CORE VALUES AND DEFINE YOUR WHY

The two foundational steps of the Realign process segment help you understand who you are, where you are, what you want, and why. I strongly recommend you spend some quality time on these steps, especially the first time you engage in this. Getting this right and defining these core components will be essential to achieving your desired results. If you're going to build a new residence for your soul, you want a sound foundation. Don't build your house on sand, and don't embark on a reinvention journey without knowing your core values and your why intimately. Investing in this work will provide you with the clarity you'll need to take your next steps in the right direction.

KNOW YOUR CORE VALUES

Who are you? What do you believe? What do you hold dear? Why do you want what you want? What drives you? What makes you *you*? The simple answer to those questions is this: your core values.

Understanding and incorporating your core values as the foundation of this process is critical. The true basis of living a why-centered lifestyle is *knowing*—and, more importantly, *living*—your core values. Therefore, this is the first step to gaining reinvention clarity. Our core values define what we stand for, and they consciously and unconsciously guide and motivate our behavior.

My why and my core values are inextricably linked. They drive, support, and reinforce each other. They simply differ in that my why may change and evolve many times throughout life's journey, but my core values almost always remain constant. A cardinal rule is that your why and core values should never be out of sync. Ensuring this alignment is an excellent way to check if your why actually fits as a key driver for your reinvention goals. If they do not align, you need to work on clarifying what your core values really are. If you focus only on identifying your why but can't articulate your core values, you're missing something critical in the equation.

We'll spend some time in chapter 3 discovering, defining, and document-ing your core values, and I will share mine with you. When you know and understand my core values, you'll know a lot about me and who I am. You'll be able to differentiate my core values from my why, but you should also readily see how they always support each other. Knowing my core values should also explain a lot about the way I've chosen to live my why-centered lifestyle and what motivated me along the way.

Why spend even one moment building a life that doesn't celebrate and affirm who you really are?

DEFINE YOUR WHY

I keep my why in the forefront of my mind and my heart every day. I wear it like an imaginary amulet around my neck close to my heart. It speaks to me, and I listen. It inspires me, protects me, and keeps me honest. I treasure it.

Since I intentionally keep my why close as my constant companion, I take notice when it begins to change, evolve, or point me toward a new des-tiny—both literally and figuratively in my case! The secret is attentively listening to my why, what it's telling me, and becoming attuned to changes both big and small. By doing this, I stay in harmony with what may be call-ing me to realign or reinvent, remain true to my purpose, and find true joy.

My why and I are old friends. I've always been aligned to it, even when I didn't know what that really meant. I've been developing and nurturing this relationship with my why ever since I was a young girl. It's like my imagi-nary friend walking by my side. Even though I always keep this friend pres-ent and close to my heart, sometimes it still becomes unclear or blocked. Sometimes it can become an elusive creature. Whenever that happens, I search for the outlines of my why in the fog, and it may take the form of a mirage in the distance I can't fully identify or define. Seeing the outlines of my why aims me in the right direction and allows me to continue devel-oping clarity as the images come into focus. This approach makes me feel more confident and less fearful as I discover the clarity I need, knowing I'm on the right track as I confirm and commit.

I believe it's a ridiculous waste of the precious time you have on earth to wander off and live in the opposite direction of your why. In this step of the process, you'll spend some time enabling the mirage to reveal itself and your why to become clear. Achieving this clarity is a critical part of any reinvention journey to find true fulfillment.

> I keep my why in the forefront of my mind and my heart every day. I wear it like an imaginary amulet around my neck close to my heart.

REINVENT: FIGHT FEAR WITH FACTS AND MAKE A PLAN

These two steps of the Reinvent segment of my process will help you find the courage and knowledge you'll need to commit to your reinvention path. The related tools and tips will give you what you need to grow, learn, and change to live the why-centered lifestyle you've clarified and envisioned.

These steps require time, effort, and energy to complete. Your investment in these steps is important because it can impact not only the outcome but also the quality of your reinvention journey. These steps can be scary and challenging but also exciting and empowering. The results will give you the essential ingredients to reach your goal.

FIGHT FEAR WITH FACTS

Fear is a reinvention motivation buzzkill. I know. As I navigated each of my reinventions, I often shook with terror. I was often afraid to let go of the life I knew, even if it was no longer serving me. Failure, losing possessions or friends, or putting my safety or security in jeopardy panicked me. I was afraid of hurting myself or hurting others. What if I wasn't good enough, athletic enough, smart enough, tall enough, experienced enough, or strong enough? What if I wasn't worthy of my dreams?

Fear keeps us stuck and saps our will. It lies to us and can be quite convincing! It has enabled so much misery and pain in our world. We lose so many opportunities because of fear, but it can also motivate us to seek change. In chapter 4, we'll discuss more about the effects of fear on living your why and how to manufacture, through knowledge, the courage to achieve the reinvention results you seek. I'll also introduce you to a visioning technique to help align your thoughts, feelings, and memories with new situations that enable progress. As your vision becomes clearer, your fears can be diminished or even become irrelevant.

We find courage not by ignoring our fear but by pressing ahead despite it.

MAKE A PLAN

Reinvention is *hard*, and it can be scary. It requires dedication and commitment to a goal. The old saying "If you love what you do, you'll never work a day in your life" is a total crock. Be prepared for lots of hard work. If living your why were easy, everyone would be doing it! Once you're armed with all the research to fortify you as you proceed, you'll need a plan. Yes, rebels make plans!

One of my favorite defense-industry mentors once told me, "Hope is not a plan." That always stuck with me. A reinvention without a plan is just a hope. It takes as much time and energy (and even more) to hope and wish for the outcome you dream of as it does to plan and prepare for it. A realistic researched plan will undoubtedly give you better and faster results with less risk. I'll help you form your research into a viable plan with related actions and timelines.

As you prepare to execute your plan, you'll take inventory of your skills and life experiences that are relevant to achieving your reinvention objectives. You may be surprised how many of your skills can be repurposed in new ways to achieve new goals. This examination will also enable you to identify where you may have skill gaps or need additional experience, support, or training to implement your plan. This gap analysis will also reveal whether you can or should seek to gain those skills or experiences yourself or if you should bring in outside help from coaches, mentors, employees, professionals, and other experts, depending on your needs.

We'll also build your personal support system into your plan. Reinvention can be grueling, and you'll benefit from having cheerleaders in your corner who care about your dreams and goals as much as you do. Your vibe attracts your tribe!

REPEAT: STICK WITH IT AND LISTEN TO YOUR WHY

The two steps of the Repeat segment of my process provide strategies and techniques to help you confirm your plans, overcome setbacks, celebrate your successes, and identify when it may be time to embark on your next reinvention journey.

STICK WITH IT

Fear is a reinvention killer, but so are apathy, frustration, distraction, and crisis. To achieve your desired results, you'll have to be persistent and be prepared for setbacks. Stick with it, and you'll get to your destination.

Once you have a plan and you've assembled the support you'll need to implement it, this step will help provide accountability. That same favorite defense-industry mentor of mine also taught me another valuable lesson. A plan is not a plan unless the related actions have someone assigned and accountable to complete them, and the due dates are set, tracked, and enforced.

Chapter 5 will provide tips and tools to keep you motivated and to help track your progress. I'll also provide examples of how I pushed through challenges, obstacles, and crises, including the strategic planning approach that I used successfully during the height of the COVID-19 pandemic.

LISTEN TO YOUR WHY

Part of my process is to revel in the new why-centered life you've worked so hard for! Wearing your rebel queen (or king) crown with pride is an important step. Recognize the purpose and joy you feel when you are living your why! You put in the work, did your due diligence, executed your plan, and stayed the course. How do you know when you've arrived? Listen to your heart. Is it singing?

Check in with your why regularly. Is it shining steady, or is it dimming, changing, swerving, or expanding as you learn and grow? Do you need something more or to move in new directions? If the answer is yes, go back and touch base with your core values and define your why to seek clarity and determine if it's time to repeat the process.

Don't get complacent. Remember, your comfort zone is where dreams go to die.

This step is too often overlooked, and it's the step that makes this concept a lifestyle. Once you've worked so hard to reinvent yourself, why would you want to look toward the next reinvention already? It's because reinvention is a continuum, not a destination. This part of the process helps you stay in tune with and in relationship with your why and hear it loud and clear. Listening closely and realigning accordingly as it changes and evolves is the true secret to living a why-centered lifestyle as opposed to just having a "second act." This is the maintenance part of the process.

Reinvention is best experienced as a series of realignments over a lifetime that enable us to live our best lives every day. And there's no time like the present to start!

Are you ready to rock and roll, rebels?

CHAPTER 2

2 | MY CORONATION AS
REBEL QUEEN
OF REINVENTION

...

I realize owning the crown as the Rebel Queen of Reinvention is a huge stake to claim, but I do have the goods to back it up. As I've created and lived my why-centered lifestyle, I've undertaken ten life-altering, renewing, and transformational reinventions (so far). Many have doubted me or thought I was crazy, but the rebel queen in me never let that stop me, and it never will!

As we embark on this adventure together, let me start by explaining a few of my key terms I'll use in this book and what they mean to me.

REBEL QUEEN

A rebel queen is born to rule. She must dig deep, overcome adversity, fight her fears, stick to her guns, and lead from the front. She is no damsel in distress. She takes the reins of her life and forges her distinct path. A rebel queen does what works for her in her own unique way, despite what others think. She often breaks rules in the process.

One truly royal example is the Rebel Queen of England, Queen Elizabeth I, who charted her own course and lived her why in the gigantic shadow of her father, King Henry VIII. Her mother, Anne Boleyn, was the second wife of King Henry VIII and was publicly executed when their marriage was annulled. Elizabeth was declared illegitimate. Henry's son Edward VI succeeded him on the throne but died shortly after at fifteen. Mary I then became queen and imprisoned Elizabeth in the Tower of London, where she narrowly escaped execution on charges of supporting a rebellion to overthrow Queen Mary.

Elizabeth I ascended the throne at twenty-six following Mary's death. She inherited a real mess—a country marred by a bankrupt economy and embroiled in deep-rooted religious and political battles. During her reign, she established the Church of England, which created a moderate middle ground between warring Roman Catholic and Protestant traditions. She unified England against the Spanish, famously defeating the Spanish Armada in one of England's greatest military victories, which brought peace to her previously divided country. She created an environment where literature, drama, and art flourished. She was responsible for English exploration of the New World and the rebound of the economy, making England a world power. The Elizabethan era was considered the golden age of English history.

Queen Elizabeth I was also a prolific writer and speaker. She famously delivered these words as land forces assembled to repel the expected invasion by the Spanish Armada: "I have the body of a weak, feeble woman; but I have the heart and stomach of a king, and a King of England too." She was known as the Virgin Queen because she never married—she was married to her people. Her unconventional course was revolutionary, and the impact she had and the legacy she left for herself, her country, and the world are undeniable. She did it her way.

A rebel queen rules with a calm, confident demeanor that often hides a mass of anxieties and doubts. She knows how to fake it till she makes it. She inspires through her example and models bravery. She doesn't take no for an answer, and if she keeps getting that answer, she'll just ask a different question or do it anyway! A rebel queen may be on her throne by birthright or by being unceremoniously thrust into that role, but she must earn it to stay there. She must often make tough decisions to care for herself and others. She knows courage is not being unafraid; it's doing the right thing despite her fears.

Another rebel queen I admire is Julia Child. Her crown is metaphorical, but she rocks it! She proved you're never too old to find and live your true calling, and she never gave up on her dreams. She was a late bloomer and in no way conventional. She wasn't made for the stuffy and conservative lifestyle of her Pasadena, California, hometown. Instead, she followed her why to serve overseas as a secretary in the Office of Strategic Services (the predecessor of the CIA), where she met and married her beloved husband, Paul, when she was thirty-six. When Paul was transferred to Paris, Julia embarked on a history-making reinvention journey that would not only change her life but also change the entire world in the process. She defined her why, fought her fear, followed her bliss, and joined an all-male class at Le Cordon Bleu. She fell in love with the French and their cuisine, started a cooking school of her own, and embarked on the massive undertaking of writing a French cookbook for American cooks. She didn't give up when her book was rejected. Her why drove her to keep at it until it was recognized for its genius. At forty-nine, she published her first book, *Mastering the Art of French Cooking*, after moving to Boston.

At fifty-one, looking for new ways to share her passion for French food, Julia persuaded her local Public Broadcasting Service station to produce *The French Chef* cooking show. A show like this had never been attempted before, especially one starring a six-foot-two fiftysomething woman with a wicked wit and an unforgettable voice! She had a unique rebellious vision. She never backed down and never took no for an answer, especially when it came to who and what she loved and championed.

Her books and television shows revolutionized the way Americans cook and eat. She's the undisputed Rebel Queen of French Cuisine, and she was bold, hilarious, talented, determined, brilliant, and fearless. The impact of her why-centered lifestyle—which began in large part with an order of sole meunière and a dream—will live on through the ages. Let's all follow in her delightfully rebellious footsteps and unapologetically follow our dreams and create our own legacies!

Let me give you one more example: Joan Jett, the reigning Rebel Queen of Rock and Roll. She burst on the music scene at fifteen with her all-girl pop-punk band the Runaways. There was no model for this type of band, and they were told it would never work. It did. After the Runaways broke up, she pursued a solo career but was rejected by twenty-three different labels before becoming the first female artist to start and have direct control over her own company, Blackheart Records. In 1980, she formed her own band, Joan Jett and the Blackhearts, which still performs to sellout crowds forty-plus years later.

Joan's powerful lyrics echo in my head and provide me with endless inspiration, such as "I don't give a damn about my reputation. Never been afraid of any deviation. And I don't really care if you think I'm strange. I ain't gonna change!" Joan has also mentored and produced other female-led punk and rock bands' records such as the Germs and Bikini Kill. She's the "godmother of punk" and a rebel who did it her way, followed her why, and broke the mold forever.

My calling and my mission as Rebel Queen of Reinvention is to provide the inspiration and guidance to enable anyone to claim their own crown. Crowns are symbols of royalty and the wearer's power and authority. They also historically represent everything from victory in battle to the divine immortality of the wearer. Crowns symbolize the authority to do what you want when you want, but the wearer must also be responsible and accountable to keep it. A crown denotes legitimacy, legacy, and respect. Wear your crown proudly like the true royalty you are.

Now let me explain what I mean by *reinvention*.

REINVENTION

The term *reinvention* is thrown around when someone wants to make a career change, lose weight, or move to a new city to shake things up a bit. These examples of life changes can be transformative, but they're usually only a part of the story or just stepping stones to the real reinvention objective. Some view reinventions as doing something different after living the same way for a long time.

In my experience, reinventions are not necessarily sequential or linear. Sometimes they overlap. Sometimes they're additive or remove something or someone. Sometimes they result in a realignment or modification of some elements of your life, your environment, or your circumstances, and sometimes they completely upend everything. To me, reinvention isn't driven by the *what*, such as money, fame, geography, career, relationships, or material possessions. Merely chasing those things alone will not bring you the transformative and lasting results you really want.

Truly meaningful and life-altering reinventions are always driven by the *why* and focus on feeding your soul rather than your wallet or your ego. Lifestyle reinventions are the deliberate result of the decision to stay in tune with your why as it evolves and to change yourself and your situation(s) accordingly.

Last, let me explain what I mean by the term *why*.

YOUR WHY

Your why is like the needle on a compass. Your why will always point you in the direction you're meant to travel. It's up to you whether to take the journey or not. As you progress through life, your why can help you find your way when you're lost, and it will guide you home. It actualizes your core values.

Why is a feeling, a calling—a destiny. It's what makes you feel centered, whole, content, and authentic. Living your why is a conscious action you can take (not just once but throughout your lifetime) to remain in full alignment with what moves you and makes you feel alive. Your why is the fire that burns deep within you and reveals, enables, and celebrates the foundational elements that make you *you*.

MY WHY-CENTERED LIFESTYLE (SO FAR)

I'm the oldest of four kids, born and raised in an inner-ring East Side suburb of Cleveland, Ohio. As I grew up, I lived through my share of fun, celebration, triumphs, and opportunities as well as sacrifices, challenges, and traumas. My mother and my paternal grandmother influenced me the most during my formative years. These women could not have been more different from each other in every single aspect, but they each molded me and inspired the woman I became in so many foundational ways.

My parents married young, and I was born nine months and one day after their wedding. My father worked the day shift at a bank, and my mother worked the night shift at a hospital. My dad would bundle me up before dawn to drive to the "hospital-bittle" (that's what I used to call it) to pick up my mom after her shift, and he'd drop her off at home to get some sleep. My dad then went to work, and he would first drop me off with his mother (my Granny), who was my primary babysitter from the time I was born. My parents met on most workdays at my grandparents' house for dinner, with my dad just coming home from work and my mom getting ready to head to work. After dinner, we'd drop my mom off at work, and my dad would take me home to sleep. Then we'd do this all over again the next day.

Granny was the daughter of an immigrant mother from the Isle of Man and a railroad engineer father from Pennsylvania. She was tough as nails. Her house was my sanctuary. I stared for hours at the small framed photo on Granny's dresser of my great-grandmother as a young woman. Draped in light blue chiffon around her shoulders like a cloud, she looked like an angel. Her dark hair and steely eyes exuded strength, confidence, and resilience. Granny had those same eyes, and I could always see myself mirrored in them. A copy of that photo of my great-grandmother adorns my office wall, and I draw strength from her watchful gaze and feel her presence, although I never had the joy of knowing her. She passed away before I was born.

What I remember and treasure most about Granny was her ability to unapologetically be herself and hold herself and those she loved to extremely high standards. She ruled the roost. No one ever doubted that. I never ever saw her as a passenger in a car; she was always in the driver's seat. She was demanding and sometimes even borderline ruthless, but she was also the most loyal cheerleader and protector I ever had. She taught me so much—how to walk, talk, read, sing, kick the habit of biting my fingernails, and set the table properly. She taught me the importance of accountability and always doing what you say you'll do. The most important principle she taught me by example was that a woman can be strong, love fiercely, and make her own way in the world without apology or permission. Her example still inspires me to this day to live the Manxman's adage: "Throw me where you will and I will stand."

My mother had a different impact on my life. She's also a strong, independent, force-of-nature woman who always does everything in her own way and in her own time. My mom was the one who truly instilled in me the importance of service to others, making an impact, and living life to the fullest. Possessions never mattered. What we did, our relationships, and our experiences mattered most. We didn't have much money, but she always made sure we had opportunities to connect with and serve others through church, school, and charitable organizations such as Girl Scouts and the Red Cross. She also made sure we bonded with our cousins, extended family, neighbors, and friends to create lasting memories. Connection and service would become the foundational values that would always guide my life and form the essence of my core values and my why.

COMMON THREADS

My why evolves as I learn and grow, and I expect that will continue until the day I die. Each time I've undertaken a reinvention, there was a distinct, underlying why that drove me, but there were also some common threads in all my reinventions:

- I live my life based on my core values. We'll talk more about that later. I know and understand them intimately, and they run through my bloodstream. I innately know when I'm living in alignment with them and can immediately feel if I'm getting off track. My core values are my guiding star, my touchstone, and they make me *me*. My why shifts and evolves, but my core values never change. That's how I know the difference between the two.

- Without exception, once I clarify and internalize my why and do the research to fight my fear, I fully commit to that reinvention and leap! I don't waste another moment. Doing my homework and making a plan have always been my major fear and doubt busters. That's why they're both critical steps in my process. Once I complete those steps, I always feel empowered to take the calculated risk of reinvention confidently and without delay.

- My transformations, although distinct and unique, were all built upon and intertwined with each other purposefully. Many of my skills and experiences were repurposed for the next reinvention to achieve my goals. Doing a skill set inventory as a deliberate part of my plan also enabled me to see where I may have gaps to fill so I could address them accordingly by building my team and/or educating myself.

- Creating opportunities for service to my community and my country has been a way of life for me. I feel peaceful and happy when I serve a greater purpose beyond myself. Finding and taking my place as a contributing member of our intertwined society always enables me to identify and codify my why and feed my soul.

- I always have an open heart and open ear when I listen to my why to see what may be shifting or calling me to move in new directions. I always remain in tune with my why, which has helped me minimize the amount of time and energy I spend living in discord with it. This has taken a lot of practice, but the more I do it, the easier it gets to feel and respond to those shifts. Realigning with my why is always more productive and fulfilling than denying it or fighting against it.

Now let me walk you through the twists and turns of my why-centered lifestyle! To date, using the process I lay out in this book, I've reinvented myself and my circumstances no fewer than ten times, following my why and leading the life I was destined for.

Reinvention 1:
Foreign exchange student

I was born and raised in Cleveland and lived a typical suburban life. I was shy, geeky, scared, and intimidated about what life beyond high school would look like. I needed inspiration to imagine what my life could become.

Near the end of my junior year, I wandered into an after-school club meeting that would provide me with a lifeline. At this meeting of the American Field Service Club, I learned about becoming a foreign exchange student. Three months later, I found myself, at sixteen, spending the summer in the small Adriatic Coast seaside town of Porto Recanati, Italy. Before that, I had never been farther away from home than Western Pennsylvania. My host family welcomed me like a daughter, and they are always and forever family. I go back to visit whenever I can, and people in that small town still remember me at sixteen. When Destiny comes to stay, it's always a party! This experience opened the wide world to me and still inspires me.

I longed for an opportunity to open my eyes, my mind, and my heart to the world outside of Ohio. I was so scared to strike out on my own, but I did my research on the exchange-student program and discovered it was a way to take my first steps into an uncharted world of possibilities in a structured program with other like-minded people. I worked hard to help raise the money to cover the program costs, and I was thrilled when I found out I was going to Italy. I didn't know a word of Italian, so I did my homework about the country, including listening to Berlitz language records from the library to learn a few phrases before I left. (Yeah, I'm that old.) This preparatory "skin in the game" helped me gain confidence and overcome my fear of crossing that big blue ocean on my own.

My parents helped cover the rest of the cost to get me there. Looking back, I recognize and appreciate how much they sacrificed. I give them a lot of credit because they always followed my lead once I made up my mind about charting my own course.

As I learned more about the customs and beauty of my hosts, I developed an abiding love for Italy and a passion for exploration and travel. I discovered my talent for languages and developed a deep sense of wanderlust. Cleveland could no longer contain me! This reinvention opened doors of possibility for the next steps in my life that remaining in Ohio never could have. This experience paved the way for building a broader and more impactful future for myself than I would have ever thought possible without this leap of faith.

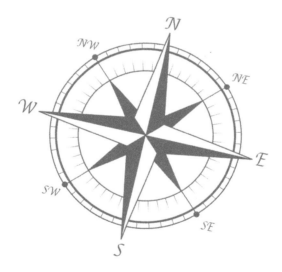

Reinvention 2:
Mae West impersonator

After I graduated from high school, I took a job at McDonald's while I was waiting to leave for US Navy boot camp (more on that later). Even after spreading my wings, pushing my boundaries, and living overseas as an exchange student to begin exploring the world, I was still a timid girl who lacked self-confidence. To truly take on the world, I longed to have the grit, wit, and strength of my silver-screen idols such as Bette Davis and Vivien Leigh.

In school, I gravitated toward music and drama, and I loved being on the stage. I still do! Performing gave me a sense of pride and confidence, and I always felt assuming the traits of a strong character helped me to form new attitudes. Playacting can serve as a practice ground for new behaviors. The moment I turned eighteen and was eligible to do so, I took off my blue polyester McDonald's uniform and started a job delivering singing telegrams as I waited to ship out to start my Navy career.

Although I was a bit shy and nerdy, I had the natural curves to pull off choosing a Mae West-based character as my performing alter ego. I studied this amazing trailblazing woman and watched her movies. Her story and example inspired me, and I wanted to reinvent myself in the image of her wild spirit. I internalized the pizzazz of this alter-ego persona as I was beginning to take my emerging womanhood, strength, and sexuality out for a spin.

I learned so much about self-confidence and being true to myself by speaking, singing, and walking a few miles in her high-heeled shoes, sequined dress, feather boa, blond wig, and rhinestone jewelry. To this day, I reach back to my experience impersonating Mae West to tap into this enduring touchstone of confidence this reinvention gave me to express myself as a sexy, fearless, and powerful woman.

Reinvention 3:
US Navy Russian linguist

Because I was the oldest of four kids in a lower middle-class family, there was simply no money for me to go to college. Plus, my grades were "meh." I was much more interested in band, show choir, and theater, and I wasn't athletic in any way, shape, or form. I'm still not! I needed a way to break out of my hometown and begin my life on my own terms. I needed a way out and a way up.

It was my dad's idea to consider the military—an idea I initially dismissed. The more I thought about it though, the more it appealed to me. My grandfather had served in the Navy in World War II, and one of my ancestors even fought in the Revolutionary War.

We were discussing it at the family dinner table one evening during my senior year of high school, and I decided right then and there to get up from the table and go to the recruiting station to learn more. My dad got his car keys, and off we went.

When I learned more about the opportunity to become a Navy linguist and to access programs to pay for college, I made the decision to enlist. My friends thought I was absolutely nuts, but the Navy's core values ("honor, courage, commitment") fit me like a glove.

I studied Russian at the Defense Language Institute in Monterey, California, and I served as a signals intelligence analyst for the next nine years during the Cold War. This was the start of my long career in the US Intelligence Community, both in uniform and as a civilian from age eighteen until I was fifty-two. To paraphrase Tom Cruise as Maverick in *Top Gun*, I could tell you what I did, but then I'd have to kill you. I tell people when President Ronald Reagan used to say we had the foreign policy of "trust but verify" with the Soviet Union, my job was basically the "verify" part.

As a foreign exchange student, I had seen a small part of the world, and I wanted to see and explore all of it! I wanted to study languages and get a college degree. My why was calling me to make a mark and serve others, and I had little opportunity to do that staying in my Ohio hometown with no viable path to higher education. It was incredibly scary taking the life-changing step of signing a proverbial blank check over to the US government for any price up to and including my life. I fought my fear by studying the job specifications and exploring the educational and travel opportunities that service in uniform would enable me to access. I knew I had found my path.

Once again, my parents backed my play. I was seventeen when I decided to enlist, so they had to sign the Navy enlistment papers for me because I wasn't of legal age. In hindsight, they were possibly trying to get rid of me because there were three more mouths to feed behind me! Either way, I'm grateful for their support and faith in me.

My Navy reinvention gave me the opportunity to see the world, pursue a college education, and play a meaningful and impactful role in the defense of the country I love so much. I also learned I'm physically, mentally, and emotionally tougher than I thought I was—another revelation that would serve me well throughout my life.

Reinvention 4: Wife and mother

I was twenty-one and assigned to my first Navy duty station in Homestead, Florida, when I met a handsome Marine. I was engaged to an Air Force guy at the time, whom I dumped to marry my Marine instead. That's another story for another time over a glass of wine or two! We worked together and were friends, but the romantic feelings between us soon became so strong that we decided to get married just two days after our official first date. Being with him felt like coming home, and I fell hard like a ton of bricks. We jumped in with both feet to build a life together. I remember calling my mother and telling her, not only was I moving up my wedding date, but I was also changing out the groom! Once again, my parents trusted me and my judgment.

Our beautiful daughter, Aimee, was born four days after I turned twenty-three while we were stationed in rural northern Japan. From the moment she was born, Aimee has been the light of my life! Raising her to be the strong, empathetic, intelligent, and resilient woman she is has been my greatest joy, and being her mother is the best and most important thing I have ever done in my entire life.

I was born to be a mom. I'm from a large family, and I also always took care of my siblings, babysat, and did volunteer work with kids. I dreamed of having a family and a child of my own. My why for reinventing myself as wife and mother was the fulfillment and comfort of sharing my life with a partner and raising a child together. This provided all three of us with mutual stability and support as our family unit explored, learned, loved, and grew together.

My Marine and I made the deliberate decision to have one child. With a military lifestyle, we felt we could focus on raising one child well within the constraints and challenges that our environment and nomadic lifestyle created. This decision allowed me to have the time to meet my military obligations while also having time to be a devoted and involved mom. I served as a Girl Scout troop leader, school trip chaperone, PTA officer, soccer game sideline cheerleader, and marching band drumline mom. For the next twenty-five-plus years, my why-centered lifestyle focused on living in partnership with the man I loved and my

lifetime job of raising the most wonderful daughter I could ever imagine.

My greatest joy

Reinvention 5: Naval officer

When my Aimee was three, my Marine left the Corps to focus on college and be a stay-at-home dad. I reenlisted in the Navy, and after seven years of hard part-time work at night, I earned a bachelor's degree in business and management. I was now the primary breadwinner for the family. Armed with a college degree, I applied for a highly competitive promotion opportunity through a Navy commissioning program. I was selected for the program and went through Officer Candidate School when I was twenty-eight.

I've never been the type of person who was satisfied with the status quo. I'm always striving to do more, be more, and serve more. The more confident I became in my ability to follow my bliss and live my why, the more I sought to do it.

I remember the night before I submitted my application for Officer Candidate School. I was super nervous and wondered if I could be competitive in this very demanding program. I told my Marine that once I submitted my application, I was committed to doing this no matter what, and we made the family decision to do whatever it took to meet this challenge. I also wanted to make a more significant impact with my commitment to uniformed service because I had gone as far as I could go in my Navy career as an enlisted sailor. To continue to advance and contribute at a higher level, I had to take a step like this to create the opportunities I needed to excel and make my mark in the US Intelligence Community.

I wasn't your typical officer candidate. If you ever watched the movie *An Officer and a Gentleman*, you might know what I'm talking about. I went back to boot camp again, but I was ten years older than the last time! I was absolutely intimidated and terrified running in tight formation alongside

Navy SEALs in my class and studying topics such as mechanical engineering and celestial navigation. Even though I was one of the shortest and oldest people in my class, I worked hard, leaned in, and did my best. Much to my great surprise and delight, I won the Leadership Award for my class as well as the award for the top officer candidate. You never know what you're truly capable of until you give yourself the opportunity to find out.

During this reinvention, I went from being a "worker bee" to being in charge, sometimes leading the same enlisted sailors I had served alongside. This was a tough transition at first, but with the help of my chief petty officer mentors, I soon got my sea legs, so to speak. This reinvention also taught me that it's good to be the boss—another lesson that's served me well throughout my life.

This reinvention cemented my decision to make the US Navy a career, and over the next eleven years, I was fortunate to have many challenging and impactful intelligence assignments as a Navy cryptologic officer. I even finished a master's degree in public administration shortly after a combat zone deployment to the Middle East. I was so fortunate to have many amazing assignments as a US Navy officer that have made significant and lasting impacts on and enhancements to our national security. Before I knew it, I had completed twenty years of service, and I was ready to hang up my **uniform and embark on new adventures in the civilian world.**

Reinvention 6: Corporate executive

I retired after twenty years and twenty days of active-duty Navy service, and I directly parlayed my military experience, security clearance, and reputation into a new civilian career in the defense industry. I focused on business development and capture, engineering, strategy, and marketing. Over the course of the next thirteen years, I worked at mammoth firms (including IBM, Northrop Grumman, and General Dynamics) in positions of increasing responsibility. Working in the defense industry gave me the opportunity to directly leverage my experience in uniform and continue making an impact on our national security in the US Intelligence Community. As I progressed to more senior positions, I was making a ton of money. This was good for our bank account, but it was also a high-pressure grind. I achieved balance in my life through mostly "mom-centric" community service and volunteer activities in my free time that kept my soul afloat.

When I retired from active duty, I was truly ready to stop uprooting myself and my family by moving to a new duty station every three years or so. My Aimee was in the sixth grade, and I wanted to plant some roots for her sake. Being a "military brat" is not an easy life for a kid. (Military families also serve.) That was a major component of my why in this reinvention. My Marine was still going to school, and I continued in my role as primary breadwinner for our family. My why, therefore, also included my need to be able to continue supporting my family after leaving the Navy. I had the education, security clearances, and relevant expertise that enabled me to choose any number of career paths. I chose marketing, strategy, and business development in the defense industry because it stirred my core value of connecting with and serving others.

I continually sought opportunities to learn, grow, and lead in my corporate role to keep my interest and to ensure I was making an impact. However, as my why in this reinvention quickly became more of a what (making money), I soon found this reinvention outcome to be exhausting and soul sucking. Although it was nice not living paycheck to paycheck as I had during my Navy days, I ultimately discovered that being on the corporate hamster wheel just wasn't for me. I learned a valuable lesson: money isn't everything. This reinvention also taught me the difference between reinvention led by the *why* rather than the *what* and that the former was much more powerful and fulfilling than the latter. I also learned to be more in tune with my why as it changes and evolves to know when the needle of my compass shifts and my alignment with my why gets out of whack.

Reinvention 7: Divorcée

I experienced a devastating but amicable divorce after a twenty-six-year marriage. This reinvention wasn't of my choosing, and it was my most upending one.

Our Aimee had just graduated from college and moved back home to figure out her next steps. My Marine had just completed his doctoral degree in education and accepted a tenure-track associate professorship in South Dakota. When he accepted the position, we made the family decision I would stay behind in Virginia and continue working for the first school year of his new job to provide family and financial stability. The plan was that I would join him in South Dakota once he settled into his new career and after our Aimee took her next steps into the world.

I thought this plan would provide the opportunity I needed to finally move out of the corporate world and allow me to explore and rediscover myself and my why. I was thrilled about that! I thought I'd finally have the luxury of not being the breadwinner—not having to carry that burden and being able to chase my own dreams. We moved him out to South Dakota just before the fall semester began in August. When I went to visit him about a month later, it was obvious something significant had changed in our relationship. The visit was strained and painful. Even after that experience, it was a surprise and a gut-punch when my Marine came home for Thanksgiving and asked for a divorce. We'd been steadily growing apart since our Aimee left for college, and we were both unhappy, but my loyalty to him was still absolute. I guess I can blame Granny for that. He was the one who mercifully pulled the plug.

During this period of extreme adjustment, I often cried in the shower. I would repeatedly say to myself that if my marriage was over, that meant my life was over. I just didn't know anything else because I had spent more than half my life as this man's wife—over a quarter of a century. At first, I just couldn't even wrap my head around it. I'd unconditionally trusted in my marriage. When it ended, I initially felt like all the oxygen was sucked out of the room, and I couldn't breathe. I'd always believed my marriage would be there as my foundation, just like I believe there will always be air in the room. When I realized that air wasn't there anymore, it took some time for me to learn how to breathe and trust again.

Although my Marine asked for a divorce for his own reasons, he did me a great favor. This life-altering event gave us both the opportunity to truly shake things up and realign to our own individual whys because we gave each other the gift of letting go.

At first, I resisted this opportunity to reinvent myself. I was initially paralyzed by denial, anger, and fear. After some time for rest, reset, and reflection, I realized this was just the beginning of a great adventure of rediscovery of parts of myself that had become numb or dormant as my marriage was dying. I deliberately decided not to carry any baggage from my marriage into the rest of my life. I'm so sad when I see so many people who poison their own lives and the lives of those around them because of the anger, animosity, regret, and hurt they carry forward with them after divorce. You can't control or change what others do, but you can control how you react to it and what you do next. Do yourself a favor and release yourself from self-imposed shackles.

This was the end of a long, long road, and the timing of this ending was not of my choosing. As I stood at this crossroad with many new options, feeling both excitement and trepidation, I had to choose a new path and move forward. Exploration, rediscovery, and reemergence of my true self on my own terms became my why.

I remain incredibly grateful for my marriage and especially for our amazing Aimee. I'm so glad I made the decision to let go of the self-inflicted fear and resentment from my divorce that I carried for a little while. The freedom that self-kindness created opened a whole new world of reinvention possibilities for me.

Divorce can truly be a gift. I know mine was! As I started to make why-centered lifestyle plans for my new life and fight through my fear, I was finally able to breathe deeply again and trust myself. I also learned the valuable lesson that being single is so much better than being in a relationship that fills your heart with doubt.

Reinvention 8: Volunteer firefighter

When my Aimee left for college, I became disconnected from many of my community service activities. Because connection with and service to others is such a foundational part of my core values and my why, I felt great discord and unhappiness. Eventually, I just didn't feel like myself at all.

After the dust settled from my divorce, I knew I needed an all-encompassing community service gig to "find my groove" and rediscover my true self. On the suggestion of a dear friend, I found the perfect opportunity and joined my local volunteer fire company! I initially served as an administrative member to help with support tasks such as fundraising and community outreach. It was awesome! They asked me to start an honor guard using my Navy skills and experience again, and in doing so, I got to interact with the operational volunteer firefighters. The more I learned about the fire service, I realized its paramilitary environment fit me like a glove. I decided to request assignment as a probationary operational firefighter and begin the rigorous training that required.

As a five-foot-three forty-seven-year-old woman, this seemed crazy, but the fire company and its leadership had faith in me and gave me a chance to prove myself. I jumped in with both feet and gave it my all. In our company, the volunteer firefighters worked night and weekend duty shifts, with career firefighters working the weekday shifts. The volunteers ran the same calls and completed the same training and certifications as the career firefighters. The only difference was we didn't get a paycheck.

I vividly remember my first training drills in turnout gear, which weighed about eighty pounds. We routinely conducted drills where we had to be fully dressed in gear and on air in less than two minutes. When I initially tried to do this, I couldn't even get myself off the floor. How could I be a firefighter if I couldn't even stand up in the gear, let alone throw and climb ladders or pull fully charged hoses? Fortunately, my crew ran me through my paces every single shift, and I soon gained the strength and skills needed to succeed with their help and support.

I'll never forget the feeling of accomplishment and purpose coming to the aid of people in my community in crisis and need. And I'll always remember the rush of hearing the tones drop and riding backward in the cab of the engine with lights spinning and sirens blaring. I'll also never forget the camaraderie of this group of extraordinary everyday heroes I was lucky enough to be part of. Riding fire trucks was an absolute blast! It kicked my ass, but those were some of the best times I ever had with some of the best people I ever met. I was truly making a difference again.

My primary why of this reinvention was that I knew I needed to be part of something bigger than myself to feel like myself again. I needed to commit myself to something that helped others and impacted lives in a positive and purposeful way. I also knew I needed to do something big and bold! Some of my prior reinventions were more about resetting or reorienting my life around a new or evolving why, but this time, I was embarking on a total renovation and renewal of the entire foundation of my life after divorce. I needed to fully reconnect with my core values to break through my fears. Serving as a firefighter, I was not only just fighting my fear of heights and confined spaces, but I was also fighting the fear that I might not recover from the trauma of my divorce.

I spent a total of five years in the fire service, with two of them riding fire trucks several times a week in addition to my full-time corporate job. Through this extraordinary experience, I found the courage to completely start over to rediscover and rebuild the why-centered lifestyle I desired. I remembered and rediscovered what made me *me*, and I leaned into it. As a bonus, I also remembered I'm a total badass.

Reinvention 9: Entrepreneur and winery owner

For years, I dreamed of owning a "someday business" in the hospitality industry. I had always enjoyed dabbling in food and wine as I traveled the world, and I envisioned a small restaurant, teahouse, or bed-and-breakfast in my future. How-to books that fed this dream and spurred ideas filled my shelves. When I turned fifty, about three years after my marriage ended, my full-time (and then some) job in the corporate world was grinding me down, and I had to admit to myself that I was getting a little too old to keep climbing on fire trucks. I decided I needed to totally recalibrate my life to my why again. I needed to blow it up.

To get started, I treated my two sisters, my Aimee, and myself to a Las Vegas trip for my milestone birthday. We lived like total ballers for an amazing long weekend. My ulterior motive for this trip, however, was gathering my girls around me as I explored and reconnected with my why and my next steps. During that trip, I decided to create an exit from my stressful life in

the corporate world. I chose to move back to my hometown of Cleveland to be near family, reconnect with my roots, and start my dream business. What an equally terrifying and exciting prospect!

Once I made that monumental decision, I bought a house in Cleveland, started doing my homework, and planned my move. I got right to work on my business plan to determine what business model was most feasible. Doing this homework was the only way I was going to fight my fear and generate the confidence I needed to walk away from my big corporate job—and paycheck. My why was calling, and I needed to chase the opportunity for connection and fulfillment I saw through opening and operating my own business. I wanted to bring something new and special to my hometown.

After analyzing the Cleveland market, I decided I didn't want to wade into a red ocean of competition with a restaurant. I love the brewery culture here and figured if it worked with beer, it could also work with wine! Over the course of the next year and a half, I created and launched a craft brewery-style urban winery concept in a hundred-year-old former auto repair garage, bringing the concept of "Good wine made fun that celebrates Cleveland and creates community" to life! I specifically built the tenet "Drink wine and do good" into the business plan and model, ensuring myself a platform for philanthropy and community engagement within my new role as business owner. I knew I would need this element to feed my soul as I took on the challenging task of running a business.

I officially left the corporate world behind three weeks before my business opened its doors for the first time. Creating an urban winery from the ground up and learning how to run it has been quite a roller-coaster ride, especially with the challenges of COVID-19 thrown into the mix the last few years. Despite all that, this reinvention reminded me it's good to be the boss! I've found immense joy and purpose bringing this community asset to my beloved Cleveland. I've also discovered that a genuine entrepreneur is less afraid of failure than of having to go back and work for someone else!

For this reinvention, I knew I needed a major reset—not just a tweak—to reconnect with myself again after a demoralizing divorce and a stressful thirteen-year run in the corporate world. I'd really lost my purpose during that time, with the notable exception of the partial (but incredibly impactful) reboot of my spirit serving as a volunteer firefighter. My age had started to get in the way of my physical ability to continue in the fire service, and I had to face the reality that I needed a full-blown reinvention this time.

My business plan came together, and I was so inspired by the architect's drawings of what that dirty old garage could look like transformed into a working winery and tasting room. I was sold but still scared shitless when I signed the lease for my five-thousand-square-foot brick-and-mortar space because I knew that was the point of no return. There was no going back. I was all in.

As I built out the business plan and prepared to invest my life savings (and a lot of borrowed money too), I thoroughly researched the hospitality industry and reflected on what I loved most about food and wine. I discovered what I genuinely loved was the connection food and wine create between cultures, within communities, and between people. That's what I wanted to build: a community center that makes and sells wine as the catalyst to bring people together—a place to celebrate, to launch dreams, to build relationships. This approach is what keeps me aligned to my why of connecting with and serving others as I run the winery day-to-day. It also helps to feed my passion for my business when the going gets a little rough.

While I'm in business to make a profit, the reason I've stayed in business is how I feel bringing this unique platform for meaningful connection and community service through wine to my wonderful hometown.

"Drink wine and do good."

Reinvention 10: Author, speaker, and coach

After six years in the wine business and as I approached my sixtieth birthday, I began to feel a strong calling to document and share my Rebel Queen of Reinvention story and my "Reinvention for Rebels" process. I wanted to share my expertise, tools, and experiences to help others achieve their own transformational reinventions and lead their own why-centered lifestyle.

I'm an experienced and polished communicator, and I gave thousands of briefings and presentations during my military and corporate careers. I also excel in translating complex technical subjects into accessible and understandable messages with the value proposition front and center. As I launched and ran my urban winery business, I heavily leveraged my communications and marketing skills. I did a lot of print and television media interviews and joined a host of professional and networking groups. I'm always in search of a platform to market my business and my vision of creating community through wine.

As I began to feel my why calling me to share my lifelong reinvention journey, I remembered how much I loved speaking, collaborating, and writing. These things light me up inside. They all channel my number 1 core value: make a connection. I started to tell my story and share my experiences with audiences large and small around Cleveland as I ran and grew my winery business. As was a factor in some of my previous reinventions, my love of performing came into play. When mentoring or coaching, I always find it so energizing to "experience share" using a Gestalt-type method of communication. This involves not telling someone what to do or giving traditional advice but instead using firsthand experiences in a comparable situation as a guide. This is a powerful way to inspire, teach, and share potential solutions.

As I learned, practiced, and grew more confident, I shared my story in local, national, and international publications, including *Cleveland Magazine*, *The New York Times*, *Wine Enthusiast*, *Decanter*, and *Forbes Magazine*. I was also blessed to meet and work with phenomenal author and speaker Kerry Hannon, who kindly wrote the foreword for this book. My midlife entrepreneur story is featured as chapter 3 in Kerry's book *Never Too Old to Get Rich*, "Military to Merlot." I've appeared as a guest on numerous podcasts, and my life and entrepreneurial journey was the subject of an award-winning documentary by Heartland Productions, *Creating Community Through Wine: The CLE Urban Winery Story.*

My story of how I became the Rebel Queen of Reinvention was really resonating with a lot of people, and that really inspired me to shout it from the rooftops! The real ignition point was when I was invited to give my first keynote address about reinvention to a large networking group of professional women in Cleveland. That experience kicked my calling into high gear. My why was not necessarily changing. It was broadening and deepening, and I authored this book because of that calling.

I initially didn't think I had the juice to take on a project like this. I was scared and even felt some shades of impostor syndrome. To fight through this fear and doubt, I hired a business coach and consulted with successful author and speaker mentors such as Kerry Hannon. I started drafting this book and seeking out speaking engagements to give me the platform I would need to further share my story to a local, national, and even international audience. This book flowed from my soul like a waterfall, and my why clarified and strengthened with each chapter I wrote. I didn't know anything about the publishing world, so I hired an experienced editor to develop a plan to publish this book. The more I stuck with it, the more I realized my message was truly revolutionary, and I had to share it!

Writing this book is my "current" reinvention experience, although I know that it will not be my last. It's important to note that I didn't embark on this reinvention because my why had *changed.* I undertook this reinvention because my why had *expanded.* My why—which led me to create a community center that makes wine in my hometown—is still intact and as strong as ever. As I have grown and learned more about myself and living my why as an entrepreneur, I strongly felt called to do more, to serve more, and to share the lessons I've learned to help others.

Another key point I learned here is that reinvention doesn't necessarily require you to leave behind everything to build something brand-new. A reinvention like this one can instead be additive to create new and complementary avenues to feed your soul. Living my underlying and interrelated whys is where the rubber has really met the road as speaker, author, coach, and small-business owner to preach reinvention as a lifestyle.

REBEL QUEEN CHAPTER WRAP-UP

I consider myself blessed to be living this life I've imagined, built, and fought for. I've made mistakes, but I've also made magic. I've made an impact, and I'm building a legacy I'm proud of. I've learned, seen, and done so much, but there's so much more to learn, see, and do! My why and I still have a lot more to offer this world. I can hardly wait to see what's next.

There's no right way or wrong way to do this. There's just your way. You have an unlimited number of times you can—and should—realign and reinvent your life whenever your why changes, shifts, or evolves. The more you do it, the more easily and readily you'll recognize the internal discord when your alignment with your why gets out of sync. You'll continue to build confidence and overcome the fear and doubt to realign and reinvent as needed through repeated self-renewal.

Reinventions don't have to be huge uprooting changes, although some-times they need to be. They don't have to be sequential. They can overlap and intertwine. I know I have more reinventions ahead of me as I follow my why's lead. You make (and can break) the rules to chart the course for your own why-centered lifestyle.

It's all in your capable hands.

AS YOU EMBARK ON YOUR REINVENTION JOURNEY,
CLARIFY WHAT IS CALLING
AND DRIVING YOU.
THIS INVOLVES THE KEY STEPS
OF KNOWING YOUR CORE WHY.
VALUES AND DEFINING YOUR

THESE PIECES OF THE PUZZLE CREATE A SOLID
FOUNDATION TO CHANNEL THE MOTIVATION, PASSION,
AND FOCUS YOU'LL NEED FOR TRANSFORMATIONAL,
LASTING, WHY-CENTERED REINVENTION.

CHAPTER 3

3 | REALIGN

. . .

I n this part of the process, you'll gain the clarity needed to guide your reinvention journey. We'll deep-dive into the critical importance of knowing,
understanding, and being centered in your core values and then spend
some time fully defining your *why*. These two steps will be your underlying
foundation and the road map that will guide you. Exercises throughout this
chapter are designed to walk you through a step-by-step process to discover,
document, and engage your compass and set your course for the trip of a
lifetime.

KNOW YOUR CORE VALUES

My why is always linked to my core values, and my core values are the
bedrock of my soul. If you genuinely want to live a why-centered lifestyle,
it's critically important to know your core values and understand how they
drive your behaviors and help to clearly define your why.

As you start your journey, I recommend you clearly identify the top three
to five core values that make you *you*. Define and document them so you
can easily understand and communicate them. I also find it helpful to list
my core values in order of importance to the definition of my character.
This enables me to keep those traits and values most dear to me front and
center when I'm clarifying my why and reinventing or realigning to live an
amazing life I love.

I've already shared with you the highlights of my own lifelong reinvention journey and how these reinventions have helped me live an authentic

why-centered lifestyle. Allow me now to lead the royal rebel procession and share my five core values, the principles that underpin all I do and all I am. You should be able to readily see the sinew between my why and my core values.

Five Core Values that make me me

- Core value 1—*Make a connection.* This is the core value that drives me like no other. I feel strongly about connecting with people, whether one-on-one, as a community, as a nation, and as a world. I'm most fulfilled and happy when I'm engaged in efforts to meaningfully bring people together, help people succeed, and make everyone feel included, heard, seen, and valued.

- Core value 2—*Build the future.* I don't like to rest on my laurels. This core value relates to my drive to always be looking ahead, doing what I need to do today to be successful, happy, and fulfilled tomorrow. I always want to learn new things that will open new doors of possibility. I don't wait around for things to happen to me or hope that they will happen by chance. Instead, I'm driven to make things happen and to create the environment that enables me to live my why.

- Core value 3—*Achieve every day.* There's no time like the present to get things done. This speaks to my core value of doing something every day that has purpose, that furthers and actualizes my why, that teaches me something, or that helps someone. It's not in my nature to sit still. I'm at my best when I'm continually growing, improving, learning, and achieving. Once I make up my mind to do something and I've done my due diligence, I make it happen!

- Core value 4—*Be positive.* This core value is all about attitude, and attitude sets the tone for everything. I choose to be positive because that's the lens through which I view, understand, and react to my world, my obligations, my challenges, and my opportunities. I don't look at a glass as half full or half empty; I view it as refillable. A cheerful outlook also helps me and keeps me going in times of crisis, especially when I need to fake it till I make it.

- Core value 5—*Deliver!* This core value is all about accountability and my commitment to doing what I say I'm going to do. I'm a woman of my word, and my word is my bond. Trust, honor, and respect are foundational to my character.

How do you define your core values? Documenting them for the first time may seem daunting, even though you may already intrinsically feel what they are. Recording and defining them is particularly important to achieve clarity and aids in communicating them effectively to yourself and to others.

In the four-step process in the pages that follow, you'll uncover, explore, distill, and define your core values. Don't skip this step, especially if you're engaging with this process for the first time. You're creating the foundation for everything that follows. Doing this introspective work is absolutely time well spent.

I developed, defined, and refined my core values over time. With each reexamination of my why, I always go back to see if I can further clarify their definition and meaning. That reexamination helps deepen my understanding of and connection to them.

STEP 1: FIND YOUR WORDS

To begin defining and documenting your core values, make a list of words, phrases, and concepts that most describe you and your character. Here are some words, phrases, and concepts to get the ball rolling:

Make your list with an open mind and an open heart. Let the words flow. Choose as many words or phrases as you need to, and don't second-guess yourself. After you've created your list, let it sit for a day or two and go back to it again, adding new ideas and removing those that don't ring true. Do this as many times as necessary to get a list that truly feels like *you*.

These are my core-value words/phrases/concepts:

_____

_____

_____

_____

_____

_____

_____

STEP 2: IDENTIFY PATTERNS

Journal your answers to the following questions, referring to your list of core-value words, phrases, and concepts created in step 1 for inspiration. You should begin to see patterns emerge that resonate with you. Dig deep and be as honest as you can when you answer these questions. They are designed to reveal those values that form your core and character.

What's most important to me in my daily life?

_____

_____

_____

_____

What are my priorities?

_____

_____

_____

_____

What positive traits do I possess?

_____

_____

_____

_____

What makes me happy?

_____

_____

_____

_____

What do I believe in?

_____

_____

_____

_____

What are my major accomplishments I'm most proud of?

_____

_____

_____

_____

What are my passions?

_____

_____

_____

_____

What's my calling or my life's work?

_____

_____

_____

_____

What activities or experiences make my heart sing?

_____

_____

_____

_____

STEP 3: AGGREGATE AND CORRELATE

Aggregate the key words, phrases, and concepts on your answers you provided to the prompts in steps 1 and 2 into three to five related groups, focusing on what resonates with you the most. After you complete the groupings, let this list sit for a while and come back to it after some additional time for reflection. Don't prioritize yet. Add, rearrange, or subtract as needed until you can feel the synergy of these groupings with your heart and soul.

Core-value words/phrases/concepts grouping:

_____

_____

Core-value words/phrases/concepts grouping:

_____

_____

Core-value words/phrases/concepts grouping:

_____

_____

Core-value words/phrases/concepts grouping:

_____

_____

Core-value words/phrases/concepts grouping:

_____

_____

STEP 4: DEFINE AND PRIORITIZE

This is the last step. Distill the content of each of your step 3 groupings into one word or short phrase that best communicates the underlying core value you're describing. Rank them in priority order now by how important they are to you and to your sense of self, fulfillment, and well-being. Add a definition for each core value, word, or phrase using the content in the previous steps as needed. This will then give you your list of three to five core values that will serve as a foundation for your why-centered lifestyle.

Core value 1: _____

Definition: _____

_____

_____

Core value 2: _____

Definition: _____

_____

_____

Core value 3: _____

Definition: _____

_____

_____

Core value 4: _____

Definition: _____

_____

_____

Core value 5: _____

Definition: _____

_____

_____

Once you've completed the four steps of this exercise, you'll have a prioritized list of core values that define your character and fuel your why. When I laid out my own core values earlier in this chapter, I included a detailed definition I've refined over time to clarify what those words and phrases mean to me. I hope I've demonstrated the power of defining what your core values mean to you so you know what behaviors and goals will enable you to live your most authentic and best life as your true self.

For example, if *faith* is one of your core values, ask yourself what that means. How is your faith manifested in your life? Your definition of faith is going to be different than mine or anyone else's. Knowing your precise definition will immeasurably help you live in alignment with your core values and your why. It's important that you understand and internalize the specific behaviors and descriptors most closely associated with your core values. This will help you tap into the changes and actions you can take to live more closely in line with them.

Don't let your core values just sit on the shelf and gather dust. Use them in your reinvention planning and find ways to keep them front and center! For example, I used my core values as the foundation that defines the culture I wanted to create in my urban winery business. I'm the owner, so I wanted to reflect both me and my why in my company culture. I wanted to operate my business in a way that would actualize my why, so I built and nurtured a company culture around my core values. Since I'm a visual person, I created a wine-focused graphic representation of my core values (shown on the next page) that helps me communicate the culture of my business to my staff and customers.

A bottle of wine is not just a bunch of squashed grapes. The term *terroir* reflects all the many and varied elements that go into making a bottle of wine, just like all the components that go into creating a company culture.

In the graphic, the grape vine represents my business, with the environment (represented by the sun and clouds) fueling the business and the core values (represented by the roots of the vine) anchoring and nourishing it. You'll notice that the definitions of the winery's core values are slightly different from those I provided earlier for myself. They're tailored here to influence the related behaviors I want to manifest in my company's culture.

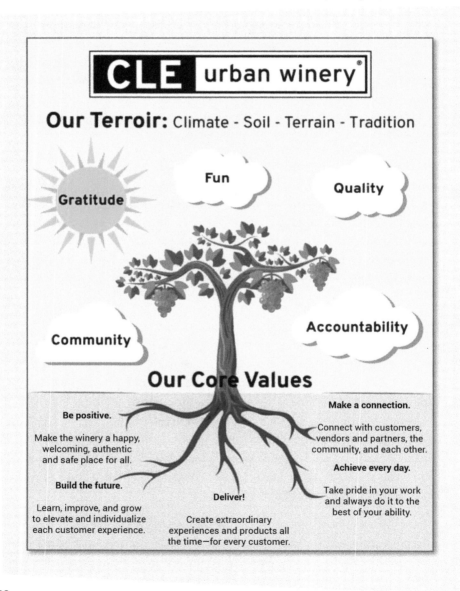

Doing this has resulted in many benefits. First, it keeps me grounded and accountable to running and building a business that feeds and honors my why. My core values give me inspiration and fuel to keep going, especially when times get tough. I know what I'm offering is authentically me, and that makes me proud. Defining the winery's version of my core values has also helped me to build and develop an amazing team of employees, vendors, customers, and supporters who understand my vision and want to help me enhance its impact and value. I use the winery's core values as a guide when I'm hiring new employees and evaluating employee performance. Because I clearly communicate how employee performance is expected to reflect these core competencies and behaviors, I can hold them accountable for operating my business that way.

Knowing your core values is so important not only to your reinvention journey but also to authentically living your life in a way that makes you happy, fulfilled, and proud as you wear your hard-earned bejeweled crown.

DEFINE YOUR WHY

Now that you have your core values firmly in mind, the real reinvention work begins.

Ask yourself:

- What do you want to accomplish?

- Who do you want to be?

- What impact do you want to make?

- Where is your soul pulling you?

And most importantly—*why*? It's time to examine and define your why.

Don't climb someone else's mountain. You'll just get to the top and be tired, empty, and cranky! Climb your own mountain, create your own life, and manifest your own desires. As any rebel knows, the dream is free, but the hustle is sold separately.

Rebels don't attach themselves to a place, a job, or a project. Instead, they align with a purpose, a calling, or a mission. The secret to success is to spend some quality time defining that mission and contemplating why the journey up that mountain will fulfill you before you lace up your hiking boots. Investing this time and effort to define your why will not only make the journey smoother, but it will also make it more uplifting.

In the remainder of this chapter, I'll provide a four-step process that will help you define your why. This is another foundational step to provide clarity about whether your current life is centered on your why or not—and if not, what direction you'll need to head as you work to change that.

PART 1: DEFINE THE WHY THAT GOT YOU HERE

First, spend some time defining your current life and thinking about how you got here. It's important to know where you are so you can get a clear picture of whether you're currently living in alignment with your *why*. There's an underlying *why* that bought you to where you are in your life today, even if it has now been overtaken by events or changes. Perhaps it was a *what* instead of a *why* that led you here. It's valuable to explore that and invest some time to reflect on it before you think about where to go next. Listen to your gut on this one; it's usually spot-on.

Write your answers to the following prompts. Be as honest with yourself as you can.

Why am I the person I am today?

_____

_____

_____

_____

Am I fulfilled? Is something missing? If so, what?

What choices, changes, or conditions created my current life circumstances?

What is my calling? How is it manifested in my daily life?

Do I feel safe and secure? Why or why not?

Am I living my core values today? If so, how? If not, why not?

_____

_____

_____

_____

_____

Now read your reflections out loud. What jumps out at you? Are you feeling any internal discord or discontent with your current life and circumstances? Were you able to identify what may be missing? Were you able to clarify some elements of your why?

PART 2: EMBRACE THE WHY THAT MOVES YOU FORWARD

Now that you've taken stock of your current alignment with your why and core values, let's take a fresh look at your why as you prepare to move forward. Put aside your current reality or situation and openly focus on what's next. Where would you go and what would you do if you knew you couldn't fail and there were no limitations?

Imagine there were no constraints on living your why, and journal your thoughts using the prompts provided. These questions will help you identify and organize your thoughts and desires as you explore, define, and clarify your why. Spend some time and attention on why you're answering the way you are. This will truly help you uncover your true heart's desire and your soul food.

What makes me feel most alive? Why?

_____

_____

_____

_____

_____

What boosts my energy? What drains my energy? Why?

_____

_____

_____

_____

_____

What makes me feel most proud? Why?

_____

_____

_____

_____

_____

What gives me purpose and joy? Why?

_____

_____

_____

_____

_____

What would I love to learn more about? Why?

_____

_____

_____

_____

_____

What am I longing to do, be, create, or accomplish? Why?

_____

_____

_____

_____

_____

Where have I always wanted to go? Why?

_____

_____

_____

_____

_____

What am I most passionate about? Why?

_____

_____

_____

_____

_____

What words most describe an awesome life? Why?

_____

_____

_____

_____

_____

_____

_____

PART 3: CLARIFY YOUR WHY

As you read through the answers you wrote above in part 2, determine what major themes jump out at you. Check back in with your answers in part 1 to incorporate any elements of your current why you want to bring forward. As you group your thoughts in the prompts below, pay particular attention and reflect on what common reasons you had for answering the questions the way you did. Living a why-centered life is not just about *what* you do but *why* you do it. Your why drives and fuels your behaviors and fulfills you. Capturing these themes will help clarify your key needs and motivations.

Theme 1: _____

_____

_____

_____

_____

Theme 2: _____

_____

_____

_____

_____

Theme 3: _____

_____

_____

_____

_____

PART 4: DEFINE YOUR WHY

Seeing your why in writing—clear, concise, and actionable—is powerful. Using the themes you synthesized, distill them even further and document and define your why here. This is the starting point as you move into the *reinvent* part of our process.

Be aware that this represents your why that you will take forward. It's important to have the clarity of this starting point so you can revisit and check in with it regularly as part of your daily life. Doing this will help you to stay aligned with it and determine if it's no longer reflecting your needs and desires or if it has changed or evolved. Always remember this is an ongoing, evolving, and iterative process.

MY WHY IS

_____

_____

_____

_____

_____

_____

_____

_____

_____

_____

_____

What should your why statement look like? Here are a few examples from my own journey to serve as inspiration:

- In my teenage years, as I began to build a life on my own, my why was about *discovery*: discovering myself and exploring the world around me, discovering my talents and how I could best use them to connect with and serve others, and discovering the confidence and courage I needed to stand on my own two feet, be an independent adult, and make my mark.

- In my twenties, as I left home, started a career, and became a wife and mother, my why was about *love*, *security*, and *legacy*. It was about building a family unit that could support and sustain me through life's ups and downs, to connect deeply in a committed relationship, to give and receive love freely and with all my heart, and to bring life into this world and build a family of my own to love and cherish.

- In my thirties, as I built my military and corporate careers, my why was about *service*, *advancement*, and *growth*. It was focused on being more, doing more, and serving more. It was also about making more money—which, in hindsight, was a what, not a why. I wanted to broaden and deepen my skills, experiences, and opportunities. I took on new challenges and chased opportunities to increase my impact through service to my country and community.

- In my forties, as I rebuilt my life after divorce, my why was about *rediscovery* and *independence*. I needed to remember who I was and what made me *me*, serve others, and reconnect with my community and my world. I also needed to assert myself as an independent woman and build a new and lasting relationship with my adult child as a single mother. I needed to find meaning again.

- In my fifties, as I left the corporate world behind to work for myself, my why was—and is—about *connection* and *freedom*. I wanted to reconnect with my family and hometown, to build something magical to bring people together and create community. I wanted to learn, serve, grow, be accountable to myself, and live and work on my own terms. I wanted to share what I've learned to help others discover their own freedom, purpose, and joy.

REBEL QUEEN CHAPTER WRAP-UP

Whew! That was hard introspective work. As you move on to the next steps in the process to fight fear with facts and make a plan, take a moment to congratulate yourself first. You've made a huge impactful investment in yourself by starting a lifelong relationship with your core values and your why that can transform you. The knowledge and insights you've gained about yourself can help you in so many ways, and what you've learned can serve as a guide and as fuel throughout your reinvention process and beyond. A new lifestyle awaits you. I'm so proud of you!

Now let's take that insight out for a spin and live a why-centered life of your dreams.

NOW THAT YOU KNOW YOUR CORE VALUES AND HAVE DEFINED YOUR WHY, IT'S TIME TO DO SOMETHING AMAZING WITH THAT CLARITY AND INSIGHT!

LET'S FIGHT YOUR FEAR AND

MAKE A PLAN

TO MANIFEST THE COURAGE AND CONFIDENCE YOU'LL NEED TO **COMMIT** TO THE WHY-CENTERED LIFESTYLE YOU DESIRE.

LET'S GO, REBELS!

CHAPTER 4

4 REINVENT

...

n this part of the process, you'll be doing the work to make necessary realignments, commit to your reinvention goals, and take actions to live a why-centered lifestyle. You'll discover how to overcome fear and doubt, craft a plan, and implement the changes in your attitude and skill set to create a life that will continually fulfill you.

What are you afraid of? Does change or instability scare you? What about failure, rejection, or judgment? Do you fear loneliness or abandonment? Losing your freedom? What if something bad might happen to you or someone you love?

Are you concerned your reinvention dreams aren't viable? Do you have the skills, resources, and experience you'll need? If so, do you know how to apply them? If not, where, when, and how do you get them?

Being frightened or intimidated about taking the necessary steps to make a change, chase a dream, and live a why-centered lifestyle is completely normal, and experiencing those fears physically and emotionally is all too real. If we just ignore those fears or seek out false comfort instead, that approach will inevitably backfire on us.

FIGHT FEAR WITH FACTS

Courage is not the *absence* of fear; it's *forging ahead* despite fear.

Ask me. I know what it takes. Even rebels are afraid sometimes; we just know how to fight our way through it. As the Rebel Queen of Aviation,

Amelia Earhart once said, "Use your fear; it can take you to the place you store your courage."

My why screamed at me so many times to get in gear and reinvent myself and align my circumstances with it. That screaming scared me every time I embarked on a new adventure. Don't you think I was petrified to get on that plane and fly over four thousand miles to Italy all alone when I was sixteen? Do you doubt my fear when I had to deliver a singing telegram for the first time in front of a massive crowd in a bingo hall? Do you think I wasn't panicked when I left the hospital for the first time with my new-born daughter and tried to buckle her into the car seat? How about when my body shook uncontrollably in my turnout boots when I had to crawl through the pitch-black confined-space maze or climb a 105-foot tower ladder while training as a firefighter? Can you imagine how terrified I was when I signed a five-year lease on a dirty hundred-year-old auto repair garage that I dreamed of turning into a working urban winery?

My fear's mortal enemy is information. I use my fear as rocket fuel to supercharge my search for knowledge and uncover the courage to proceed. Knowledge is the magic that changes my attitude and my perspective on what's possible. Armed with facts, I feel more confident when breaking the rules and following my bliss. I'm empowered to make decisions and investments that can mitigate the risks I'm taking. Relevant information reduces my doubts, uncovers new opportunities, and spurs me into action.

Have you considered that you can overcome your fear, or are you living in a way that prevents you from finding out whether those fears truly are so overwhelming? You can put that fear in its proper place by doing your homework. Become the expert in your why and on the new life you dream of. Unbiased and fact-based research is a necessity, not an afterthought. Base your actions on data and truth, not on emotions. Your fears will lie to you. They need acceptance, resignation, complacency, and repetition to survive. And when they survive, you don't thrive.

When you're afraid, you avoid situations that cause you fear and develop tricks or habits that can temporarily downplay your fears. These are normal defense mechanisms we all use. Ironically, these safety and avoidance techniques can reinforce your fears and give them power. When you act as though these fears are overwhelming, a self-fulfilling prophecy evolves that can even intensify these fears. It's also just as much (and possibly more) work to maintain this facade of avoidance rather than just facing these fears. Facts, knowledge, new experiences, skills, and support will be the springboard you need to plan and move ahead even if you're still a little scared.

With facts in hand, it's much easier to act as if you feel safe and confident, even if you're still working on that. This confidence will help you increase your tolerance for uncertainty—a major cause of worry and fear. You can't control every circumstance or situation, but you can control how you react to them. Get out of your own head and out of your own way. Fighting fear requires action to achieve new results. Focus on what you can do and let go of what you can't. This will help you resolve the issues that may be worrying you or holding you back.

In the following pages, I'll share tips, tools, and strategies I've found helpful in fighting my fears. These are not sequential processes like those step-by-step tools in chapter 3. Instead, they're elements for your toolbox that you can pull out whenever you need them to uncover the courage to live your why even if you're afraid.

TOOL 1 | *WHAT ARE YOU AFRAID OF?*

You've done the work to define your core values, and you've locked your why in the metaphorical amulet around your neck. What fears do you now have that are holding you back from implementing a reinvention plan? When exploring and understanding your fears, it's helpful to gradually, but repeatedly, expose yourself to those things you fear. This exercise will enable you to explore, document, and experience the negative emotions and feelings associated with your fears rather than avoiding them. Facing your fears in this way can help you let them go or at least make them more manageable.

1. On the left side of the prompt below, make a list of the situations, circumstances, places, or objects that you fear related to living your why.

2. Rank each item on your list from least scary (0) to most scary (10).

3. Once you have this list, start with the least scary item on it and do some research on it. Speak to an expert on it. Find ways to expose yourself to it until you start to feel less fear or anxiety about it. The more you learn and the longer you face it, the more comfortable you'll become. As you gain more confidence, move up the list to those fears that are scarier and repeat this process. Through this exposure, you'll gain facts, resources, support, experience, skills, and confidence to tame these fears.

MY FEARS   RANKING (0–10)

_____   _____

_____   _____

_____   _____

_____   _____

_____   _____

_____   _____

_____   _____

_____   _____

_____   _____

TOOL 2 | *FLIPPING THE SCRIPT*

Your feelings, thoughts, and memories can be major drivers of fear. Trying to ignore or suppress them can increase their frequency, power, and likelihood to impede you as you change your current situation for the better. Thoughts are things. To begin taking the power for yourself and from your fears, you need to allow yourself to process your feelings with purpose and control when and where you feel safe and secure.

The first part of this exercise gives you a way to view your current situation and the journey to your desired result, all while navigating the feelings generated by your current situation. It will help you identify related actions you can take to manage those feelings as you proceed. It can also show you if your current situation, mindset, and trajectory can get you where you want to go or not.

Once you have a view of where you are, the second part of this exercise flips the script to help envision and clarify ways to achieve your why-centered result. You'll create a road map to find your way by starting with the desired result and working backward to identify the related actions, feelings, and situations that can manifest new pathways to tame your fears and demonstrate what's possible.

LET'S GET TO IT!

1. Start by identifying an *existing* situation causing you fear as you make your reinvention plans. Use the prompts provided to chart your course from current state to end state, and see where it leads. Write your answers in the *first-person present tense*. As you pull this thread, the result may not be what you want or need. That's okay. Be honest and see where your current situation leads you. This is valuable information that can inform your plans. You'll gain insights into your feelings about your situation, how they drive your actions and impact your results.

What *situation* is causing my fears?

_____

_____

_____

_____

What *feelings* does this situation evoke?

_____

_____

_____

_____

What *actions* am I taking because of these feelings?

_____

_____

_____

_____

What are the *results* of my taking these actions?

_____

_____

_____

_____

2. Set aside what you wrote and go do something fun or relaxing for a while. When you come back to it, read it over silently a few times and then slowly read it out loud. This process can help lessen the anxiety this story causes. Feelings aren't right or wrong—they just are. The actions you take because of your feelings, however, are within your control. Take another look at your answers in step 1. Could different actions generate different results?

3. Now it's time to flip the script. Using the new prompts provided, write another story where you start with your desired result—the one that will align you with your *why*. Think big and without constraints. This is your dream scenario! Once you describe the result you seek, imagine the actions it will take to get you there and how taking those actions will make you feel. Then describe the ideal situation that allows you to process those feelings. Write in the *first-person future tense* this time.

This exercise in reverse engineering enables you to identify a comfortable starting point that can lead directly to your desired result if you follow your own road map through the actions and feelings you expect to encounter along the way.

At the end of this exercise, you'll have generated key insights into the situation you need to create for yourself that can fight your fear and lead to why-centered living.

What *results* will I achieve when I live a why-centered lifestyle?

_____

_____

_____

_____

_____

What *actions* will I take to achieve these results?

_____

_____

_____

_____

_____

What *feelings* will my actions evoke?

_____

_____

_____

_____

_____

What *situation(s)* will help me manage these feelings and take the necessary actions?

_____

_____

_____

_____

_____

By navigating this journey in both directions, in both present and future tense, you'll generate more clarity on the impact your fear is having on your ability to reach your goals. You'll have a better view of the actions required to fight your fear and change or modify your current situation.

This introspective information will be very helpful as you make your plans for reinvention in the process steps yet to come.

This technique can help you feel less fearful of the feelings, thoughts, and memories that may be holding you back. It doesn't, however, seek to trivialize or gloss over what happened to create them. By using this tool, you can help your fears take their proper place as something that happened in the past. You no longer need to carry this baggage into the future if it no longer serves, helps, or protects you. You've identified actions that flip the script and the anecdotal evidence that can make all the difference.

TIP 1 | *TRY ON YOUR NEW SHOES FIRST*

Don't let your fears boss you around and tell you what to do (or not to do). Shake things up and try taking some baby steps in those new shoes you dream of filling—those shiny shoes that your why is calling you to put on. Walk a mile or two in those new shoes before you buy them. Make sure they fit well before you jump off the cliff in them! Apprentice or volunteer in activities, causes, and jobs aligned with your why so you can test-drive your potential new direction. You will gain hands-on insights, experiences, and information to develop your plan and fight your fear.

When I decided to leave my corporate job and start a business, I decided I wanted to go into the wine business. Guess what? I initially knew nothing about it besides being a casual wine drinker. I was afraid of making mistakes with this major shift and huge start-up investment, mostly because I only had anecdotal information that supported my belief that I could create a community connection through wine. Fortunately, a former colleague from my defense-industry job had opened a winery. I reached out to him and his wife to see if I could spend some time shadowing them in their tasting room and assisting with a bottling run for their new vintage of wines. Spending time in those environments enabled me to do a trial run alongside people I trusted and respected who were already doing it! I saw that my dreams were possible, and this diminished my fears. It built my knowledge and confidence and fed my passion.

TIP 2 | *ASSEMBLE YOUR ROYAL COURT*

Every queen or king needs a court—the people who stand by them and support them as they rule. Create your own band of merry rebels! Building your emotional support network of like-minded courtiers is a powerful strategy to fight your fears by carefully choosing your companions for the journey who can lift you up along the way.

Whom do you know can help you, guide you, and connect you? Whom do you know can aid your research, help you access resources, and change your circumstances? Reach out to your social and professional networks to ask for help, insights, and guidance. Find mentors who can be cheerleaders and sounding boards or who can instruct you or experience-share. Let them help you lighten the load.

TOOL 3 | *FEAR FABLES*™

Many fears are based on hypotheticals, not on actual truths. These hypothetical fears, however, can still have great power over us and our thoughts, feelings, and actions. A Fear Fable is a tool you can use to generate the inspirational evidence of what's possible when you face your fears and attain your goal. Seeing your feared scenarios laid out in story form, you may realize they're not as scary or triggering as you originally thought. The power of positive visioning can lessen the grip your fears have over you.

This tool is a bit different from the other strategy I gave you for flipping the script. That approach walked you forward and backward through cascading situations, feelings, actions, and results (and vice versa) to form navigable pathways from your current situation to the results you seek. The insights you gain from that exercise, especially the feelings and actions needed to flip the script, can be effective source material for your Fear Fables. The key difference is that Fear Fables give you a mechanism to skip over the fear and, instead, imagine and describe what success looks like in vivid detail. You can craft a big-picture perspective or drill down into a specific scenario that's blocking you. Fear Fables help you uncover what's possible and put your fears into perspective.

I recommend keeping a Fear Fable journal that you can use throughout your journey. If you can imagine it, you can do it! The prompts below provide a framework. Repeat this exercise as new fears arise or revisit recurring fears with new stories of triumph and achievement. When you clearly envision the successful outcome you desire, that fear-slaying energy can give you the boost of confidence you need to get there.

What am I most afraid of or worried about?

_____

_____

_____

_____

_____

Write a story about overcoming this fear and achieving great success in the process. Be as detailed as possible, and take that leap of faith to imagine what can happen if you set aside your fear.

_____

_____

_____

_____

_____

_____

_____

_____

MY NAVY BOOT CAMP FEAR FABLE

When I joined the US Navy, which aligned so well with my core values and my why, I was equally excited and petrified. I feared all the physical and mental demands of a military career, especially since so few women were assigned to my chosen career field. Initially, I couldn't see myself in this male-dominated environment, overcoming the challenges and arduous tests I would face in boot camp and beyond, especially the ones I had seen in the movies. To face these fears, I first set aside my preconceived notions. I researched the facts, benefits, and difficulties of a military lifestyle by networking with people who had successfully navigated them. I attended workshops and training sessions led by my recruiter to help prepare me for the rigors to come. I had never been an athlete, but I implemented a physical fitness regimen that would help me persevere in this new environment.

The more I planned, the more prepared and confident I felt. Was I still scared when I boarded that bus for Recruit Training Command in Orlando, Florida? You bet I was. But because I had invested in research and preparation before I got there, I took those steps with the pride and confidence I needed to take on the challenge. When I was in boot camp and found myself afraid, I created a Fear Fable that let me imagine what would happen if my fears didn't own me. I created a detailed plausible scenario about my fear and how I overcame it rather than just scaring myself with vagaries and rumors. This allowed me to identify and experience the fear and other feelings this scenario evoked and build helpful strategies to address them.

Part of Navy boot camp is to learn damage control methods to save a ship from sinking using a simulator called *USS Buttercup*. We heard a lot about this intense training through the rumor mill. We would be trapped in an enclosed metal box with water pouring in from everywhere. The object of the training was to work together to plug the leaks or else go down with the ship. This sounded terrifying! The Fear Fable I created detailed what would happen once we were all in the simulator together and the water started cascading in. I imagined the water raining down on me from all sides and felt the fear of not knowing what to do. My shipmates and I got to work and leveraged the trust we had built with each other through our many training evolutions together. I knew they had my back, and I had theirs. I saw myself applying the knowledge we had learned in our classroom training about shipboard damage control. We plugged all those leaks like pros and saved the ship. I heard our instructors guiding us and challenging us while also keeping us safe in this controlled training environment.

After I walked around in my mind a bit with the reality of what I feared and saw how I could be successful, I wasn't quite so scared. I've used this strategy repeatedly throughout my life on my many reinvention journeys. Thoughts are things, both positive and negative, and Fear Fables can really help you shape and manage them.

MAKE A PLAN

If you fail to plan, then plan to fail.

You'll need a realistic and comprehensive plan to navigate the financial, social, logistical, and emotional implications of your reinvention. Planning isn't about eliminating risks; it's about managing them. Your plan should focus on how you can achieve your goals while you identify and mitigate potential risks. This will require thought and careful preparation that use your core values and your why as the guiding principles for your actions. Doing all the work to reach your destination without those two key ingredients as the centerpiece of your plan would be a hollow victory indeed.

In this part of the process, I will provide you with tips and tools that will help you create a road map to your desired destination. You'll create realistic steps to protect yourself and hold yourself accountable to make your reinvention happen. As the Rebel Queen of Country Music, Dolly Parton, once said, "If you don't like the road you're walking, start paving another one." Make your plan, and pave your new road.

Believe it or not, this rebel is a total process wonk. I spent many years in the military and in corporate roles leading and managing complex projects. I naturally gravitate toward proven project management tools to provide structure and accountability, and I've used them successfully in my own reinventions. These tools and techniques will help you plan your reinvention, identify the resources you'll need, inventory your skills and experience, identify any gaps, and build your support team to implement your plan. The objective here is to confirm that you're manifesting what you need to live your why as you were meant to. You may recognize some of these concepts from the Business 101 classes you might have taken in college, but I'm here to tell you these tools and tips work and can keep you on track. Yes, rebels use spreadsheets and charts.

TIP 1 | *GET YOUR FINANCIAL HOUSE IN ORDER*

As you prepare for reinvention, get in good financial shape. Your personal credit score matters a lot. Debt and bad credit are dream killers. You'll need "skin in the game." Don't expect anyone else to invest in your why and your dreams if you won't or can't. Plan, prepare, and "rightsize" your life so you can afford the cost, adjustments, sacrifices, and changes your reinvention may require. Make this a key part of your plan because it will pay dividends (literally and figuratively).

After thirteen years in the defense industry, I found myself in a place where I was living in discord with my why, and it was slowly killing me. I was divorced, my Aimee was fully launched, and I was my own sole means of support. I was making a huge salary as a defense industry executive, but I was living well below my means. Nevertheless, the thought of walking away from all that money and security to realign with my why was terrifying. I wanted to go into business for myself, and I knew that would be an expensive and risky proposition.

To fight that fear, I spent several years getting my own personal financial house in order, paying off credit cards, saving money, and beefing up my credit score. After this concerted effort, I was in a strong position to be able to make a realistic plan to live my why through entrepreneurship and open my own business. I wrote a business plan emphasizing start-up costs, risks, and forecasted revenue, overhead, and wine production costs. If you've even opened a business, you know it always costs more than you planned it would, but I did my research to create realistic estimates. I knew when I opened my own business, I would have to leave my high-paying job behind, and I probably wouldn't be able to pay myself a salary during the start-up phase. I also knew I still wanted to eat and have a roof over my head!

Since I would be investing most of my savings into my new business venture, I also knew I needed a plan to build a life in Cleveland that I could afford solely on the proceeds of my US Navy retirement pension. I purchased a modest home and built a comfortable downsized and affordable life in Cleveland. I had military service in a combat zone, so I was able to access medical care through the local veteran's hospital, further strengthening my safety net. This preparation enabled me to take the calculated risk to leave my big salary and company benefits on the table and manifest a more purposeful and fulfilling life. This plan has served me incredibly well over the years since I opened my winery, especially during the twists and turns of the COVID-19 pandemic!

Cash is king—in business and in life. Unfortunately, that's just a fact. My strong recommendation is if you're looking to make a lifestyle reinvention to live your why, especially a major one, make sure your financial house is in order first.

TIP 2 | *BUILD YOUR DREAM TEAM*

You can't implement your reinvention(s) alone. It truly takes a village! It's important to know what you know and what you don't know so you can get the help and support you need. It's critical to assemble (and some-times hire) supporters who are aligned with your core values and who are as excited about and invested in your reinvention as you are. A key part of your plan must be a self-assessment where you take stock of your transfer-able skills and experience that will help you implement your plan.

As a key part of your plan, perform a gap analysis to identify the skills and expertise you don't currently have but will need to succeed. With this analysis in hand, your plan can then include the education, internships, interviewing and hiring, and other methods to assemble your dream team to enable you to achieve your goals.

When I began planning to open my winery, I had a fully fleshed-out vision of the customer experience I wanted to provide, but I had no earthly clue how to run the back end of a complex business model like this. I hadn't even used a point-of-sale system since I was eighteen and still wearing that blue polyester McDonald's uniform. Since I never really got the knack of balancing my own checkbook, I knew I would need lots of help with finan-cial concerns to cover all the bases and stay on the right side of the IRS. I hired a payroll management company to make sure I stayed compliant with related rules, taxes, and payments. I also hired a bookkeeper and an accoun-tant to make sure I was managing the finances of the business and paying all required debts and taxes. I also made sure I had solid financial data and reporting to make sound business decisions.

After my business opened, I enrolled in the Goldman Sachs 10,000 Small Businesses program and joined the Entrepreneurs Organization Accelerator program to educate myself on all the other aspects of running a business I didn't have experience with. Since I had no idea how to make wine, I hired a kick-ass winemaker to help me implement my slightly wacky wine production concept to perfection. This was a significant investment of time and money, so lining up the expertise I lacked was crucial to implementing my plan successfully. I was able to focus on doing things I already had experience doing: marketing, branding, tasting room decor, and creating the connected customer experience. I hired employees who understood and embodied what I was trying to accomplish. Remember, I hire based on my core values—employees and vendors alike.

Focusing on what I do best and outsourcing or hiring out the rest enabled me to build a business that actualized my why and managed my risk. Reinventions can be a heavy lift, so get yourself some qualified help.

TOOL 1 | *YOUR REINVENTION PLAN*

My approach to reinvention planning is like creating a business plan. The key difference is that a business plan is used primarily to document and communicate your business concepts, objectives, and forecasts to others, including bankers, investors, and potential business partners. You use a plan like that to sell your concept to someone else. Your reinvention plan is for you. It's your touchstone, vision, strategy, road map, and action list rolled into one. You can, of course, share it with others, but it's intended to be the resource, accountability tool, and written record of everything you need to facilitate your reinvention all in one place. You'll get out of it what you put into it. Decide what kind of life you want and then say no to everything that isn't that.

The time has now come to put the proverbial pen to paper.

Intention + Action = Magic!

I believe it's essential to take the time and make the effort to write your reinvention plan down. The act of documenting your plans and strategies in writing truly helps to make and keep them real. You can create your reinvention plan using whatever formats and templates you prefer, but it should include the following components:

SECTION 1: MY CORE VALUES

State your core values and their definition from the Realign portion of the "Reinvention for Rebels" process (Know Your Core Values).

These will serve as an important touchstone throughout your reinvention planning process to ensure you remain true to yourself.

SECTION 2: MY WHY

Document your why that you clarified in the Realign portion of this process (Define Your Why). Refer to this section of your plan often for motivation!

This will provide guidance and direction for your plan. Everything in the following sections should be focused on actualizing your why.

SECTION 3: MY REINVENTION VISION

Define what living your why-centered life looks like. This section of the plan is for the overarching view of the next stop in your reinvention continuum.

Make sure your vision, your core values, and your why are connected and aligned.

SECTION 4: MY REINVENTION GOALS

Determine the principal goals and objectives you'll need to complete, from start to finish, in order to manifest your reinvention vision.

These goals will translate to specific milestones, tasks, and actions in section 6 of your plan to make your reinvention vision a reality.

SECTION 5: MY SELF-ASSESSMENT

Identify the skills, experience, and investments needed to achieve your reinvention vision and goals. Assess your transferable skill set and available resources to determine what you already have and what you need to acquire.

This information will translate to specific tasks and actions in section 6.

SECTION 6: MY ACTION LIST

Create an action list to document specific milestones, tasks, and actions to achieve your reinvention goals and vision. This list includes the major milestones to get you there, the related tasks needed to reach those milestones, and the underlying actions that must be accomplished to complete those tasks.

For each action, your list must include who is responsible for completing it and a due date to ensure accountability. Section 6 is a living part of your plan, while sections 1–5 are primarily static and included for inspiration and reference.

Do something every day to work these actions. Regularly schedule time to review, update, and status them. Remove completed actions and add new ones as they materialize throughout the process until you achieve your vision.

This is the section that makes your plan real—where rubber meets road.

TIP 3 | USE PROJECT PLANNING BEST PRACTICES

I spent years leading and managing complex projects, and I came to rely on project management best practices and tools to keep me on task. I found that many of these tools were readily transferable to managing a reinvention transformation as well. This may not sound rebellious, but using these tools has helped me tremendously when executing my own reinvention plans. This is a prime example of using and repurposing skill sets and experience you have in one area of your life to help manifest new horizons.

An example of a helpful tool to visualize your plan and its milestones is a Gantt chart, a type of bar chart that illustrates a project schedule. A Brit named Henry Gantt created this methodology in the early twentieth century. It's a graphical representation of activity against time. You can learn more about Gantt charts from the Association for Project Management (https://apm.org.uk).

The main benefit of a Gantt chart is to show a top-line perspective of a project or plan. You can also use them to allocate resources, depict schedules, and highlight interdependencies between tasks and activities. The resulting graphic representation of your plan can facilitate the accountability to complete it.

A Gantt chart can also identify your "critical path," the longest path (in time) from start to finish of a project to complete all the essential tasks. It highlights places in the plan where an incomplete task can cause a delay in the related sequence of tasks to meet project milestones, thus pushing back the project's overall completion timeline. If you have a fixed end date in mind for your plan, understanding your critical path becomes particularly important to make sure you stay on track.

A simple Gantt chart can help you create a high-level "waterfall" view of your reinvention journey to show your progress and highlight where pitfalls may be encountered. While some versions of this chart can become quite complex, you can keep it simple by just showing the major milestones, dependencies, and timing. Once all action items related to a task on the chart are complete, that related milestone is fulfilled. If actions on your list remain open, that related task and milestone do as well.

AN EXAMPLE

Here's an example tied to my vision of becoming an officer in the US Navy. The content and dates are purely representative, but it should give you the idea of what I'm talking about. Major milestones are represented in this example, along with the high-level tasks required to reach that milestone. The related actions to complete these tasks, such as completing required paperwork, were documented and tracked separately. Each task may require many separate actions to accomplish, and I chose to leave them off the Gantt chart example here to allow the critical path to be more clearly visible. I couldn't meet the deadline milestone for application submission without completing all the required underlying tasks first. It was helpful for me to see these task and milestone interdependencies to stay on track and achieve my reinvention goals and vision to become a naval officer.

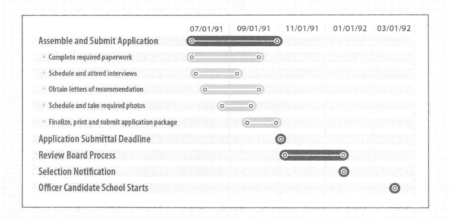

REBEL QUEEN CHAPTER WRAP-UP

Now that you've faced your fears and made your plan, your reinvention has the guidance, structure, and momentum it needs to take you exactly where you want to go. But as we all know, the best-laid plans are always going to encounter bumps along the way. I always say, "If it's not something, it's something else." The next chapter will detail the Repeat portion of my process, which will help manage setbacks and confirm your ongoing alignment and relationship with your why.

TO LIVE A WHY-CENTERED LIFESTYLE, YOU MUST BE ABLE TO
CONFIRM
WHEN YOUR
WHY NEEDS
SOME
REEXAMINATION, TWEAKING, OR EXPANDING.

THIS OPPORTUNITY FOR ONGOING RENEWAL AND REINVENTION
ALLOWS YOU TO KEEP DISCOVERING, EVOLVING, AND
LIVING A LIFE YOU LOVE
EVEN AS YOU, YOUR DREAMS, AND YOUR CIRCUMSTANCES CHANGE.

CHAPTER 5

5 | REPEAT

The one constant in life is change.
Only you can decide what to do with that opportunity.

...

You did the internal work and soul searching to tap into your core values and to clarify your why. You fought your fears with knowledge and information, you charted your course, and you made a detailed plan to get you where you want to go. Now it's time to implement that plan and commit to keeping it alive in your daily life. No sweat, right?

The pathway to a why-centered lifestyle—to paraphrase Shakespeare in *A Midsummer Night's Dream*—never did run smooth.

To truly live a why-centered lifestyle, you've got to want it—bad. All kinds of obstacles, excuses, crises, and setbacks will try to thwart you. You'll get distracted and pulled in different directions. You'll be discouraged and overwhelmed. Your courage may fail you. In this chapter, I'll provide you with the encouragement, tips, tools, and tactics that can keep you going despite the roadblocks that will inevitably pop up on your path.

My why and I were always friends and companions, but our relationship has deepened to the point where we've become BFFs. I've realized the importance of taking swift action when living in discord with my why and the consequences of inaction. I'll share my strategies and experiences for building a deep and lasting relationship with it. This ongoing dialogue has been essential to remaining in tune with my why as it shifts or expands. This enables me to continually and routinely take steps to align my lifestyle to actualize my why as the foundational part of my daily life. The rebel in me delights at the prospect of using this revelation to bring my journey full circle and offering you the opportunity to come along with me as we live our best why-centered lives.

STICK WITH IT

If at first you don't succeed, regroup, refine, and try and try again. Reinvention is not for the faint of heart, and the road is often rocky and filled with pitfalls. In addition to fear and apathy, frustration and distraction can also be fatal for your reinvention motivation. Don't let the inevitable setbacks or obstacles you may encounter prevent you from doing whatever it takes to live your why every day. In this part of the process, you'll be doing the work that will help you persevere and triumph. Remember this little equation for inspiration:

SUCCESS =
PREPARATION +
OPPORTUNITY +
PERSEVERANCE +
A LITTLE LUCK!

When I was ready to build out my winery space and needed a sizable start-up loan, the first bank I approached for financing turned me down flat. That could have killed my reinvention plans right there because getting the money to start my business was a key part of my critical path. I believed the business plan I'd poured my heart and soul into was perfection and was incredibly compelling (no bias there, right?), but the banker apparently did not agree.

Instead of taking no for an answer and giving up, I went back to the drawing board. I updated my business plan, my assumptions, and my pitch with the help of small-business mentors. I added a high-level summary coversheet to my loan application that clearly spelled out my vision and ensured it was front and center. By making these adjustments, I was able to communicate the overarching value proposition of my plan more directly and effectively to a banker in their own language. I reviewed my plan and practiced my pitch in front of people who had experience dealing with banks and could offer constructive criticism. I then took my updated plan to a new banker at a different bank, and I got the answer I wanted and the money I needed.

I always try to learn something from every success and failure. Challenges, changes, and crises can have silver linings. Everything won't always go according to plan, but that may not necessarily be bad. Resiliency, creativity, and flexibility are key ingredients in any reinvention. And don't forget the power of your sense of humor! If you want it bad enough, don't stand still. Always look for new ways to up your game, to address issues, to create better balance, or to work the system in your favor.

TIP 1 | *MAKE IT REAL EVERY DAY*

Each time I realigned with my why and reinvented myself, I made sure to do at least one thing every single day to keep things moving forward. It might have been nothing more than sending an email, having a meeting, submitting a document, making a key decision, or connecting with a resource, but it kept my plan alive and real. It also helped to sustain my motivation and my passion as well as keep my fear at bay.

Make a daily commitment to move your plan forward, work on your action list, or further your vision in other tangible ways. Each step to keep your plan moving forward, even a little bit, is time well spent. Focused and concerted effort, enforced accountability, and keeping your dream of a why-centered lifestyle in the forefront every day will become a powerful mechanism to help make your plan reality.

TOOL 1 | VISUALIZE YOUR PROGRESS

Another project management best practice that can be extremely helpful in generating and instilling accountability in your reinvention plan is a kanban board. Kanban is a Japanese method to manage work. A kanban board visually depicts work at various stages. It uses cards to represent action items and columns to represent stages of the process. This tool helps you see your work as it progresses.

A kanban board brings your reinvention plan's action list to life as you write down the actions, categorize them, and then work through them in a systematic way. You can use a spreadsheet or fancy software tools to generate a digital kanban board, or you can just use a wall or whiteboard and 3M stickies. I personally find it more compelling to see the physical manifestation of the board. Make it as complex or as simple as you want. Use whatever format motivates you, keeps you on track, and makes you proud of your progress!

Divide your board into three sections (see example below). The three columns of your kanban board should have the following headers: To Do, In Process, and Done.

- The To Do column is for actions you need to do but haven't assigned or started.

- The In Process column is for actions that have been assigned, are in work, and are actively being tracked.

- The Done column is for actions that are complete.

TO DO	IN PROCESS	DONE
ACTION 6	ACTION 3	ACTION 1
ACTION 2	ACTION 5	ACTION 7
		ACTION 4

Write your action on a card and affix it to the applicable area of the board. Write as much or as little detail about the action on the card as you find helpful. As the last column fills up, this will give you visible evidence of how far you've come and how much you've accomplished! As the Done pile grows, your confidence will soar!

TOOL 2 | *DEFENSE, STABILITY, RESET, OFFENSE (DSRO)*

When I became an entrepreneur, navigating my business through a global pandemic was not part of my original plan. I had to reach deep into my bag of tricks from my corporate days and find a way to revive, repair, and reinvent my business in this new reality. I used the four-step strategic planning concept for crises called DSRO to mitigate business loss, to overcome and recover from the disruption, and to position for the future. This crisis management strategy can be applied to navigating a comeback from any setback, with the approach tailored to the scope of the crisis.

When the pandemic hit, I went into *defense* mode. This part is about pure survival, meeting basic needs, and stopping the proverbial bleeding. On March 15, 2020, when Ohio governor Mike DeWine announced that all bars and restaurants were closing that evening at 9:00 p.m. until further notice due to COVID-19 concerns, I was stunned. After I cried for a while, I dried my tears and went on defense. I laid off my bar staff, did everything possible to cut my other overhead costs to the bone, and reached out to my network for guidance and support. I had no idea how long this would last or what was coming next. For the next three months, I pivoted like crazy to online sales and delivery, curbside pickup, and anything else I could think of to help keep my head above water. I hunkered down and hustled like crazy. No sourdough starters for me.

When the governor allowed bars and restaurants to begin reopening, there were still so many unknowns due to the COVID crisis. When experiencing a catastrophe like this, especially an upending and unexpected one, it's counterproductive to try to bounce from a defensive position straight back to offense. As the initial COVID lockdown began to ease, there was no "getting back to normal" possible at that point—no way to go straight back to fixing everything. So much was completely out of my control. That's why the next step in this approach, *stability*, is so important. In any emergency room, the priority is always to stabilize patients before you try to heal their wounds.

When we got permission to reopen in June 2020, I rehired one bartender; sanitized the winery from top to bottom; implemented new cleaning, safety, and customer service protocols; rearranged seating for increased distancing; and installed plexiglass and air filtration systems. I applied for every financial aid program I could think of. I took these steps deliberately and slowly, making small adjustments and applying the latest information to stabilize operations. I made no large moves. I kept the lights on. This phase lasted well into 2021 until vaccines became widely available. We weren't trying to recover or fix things at this point. We were just trying to do what was necessary to keep things going in this new reality and learn all we could.

Once conditions became more stable and we had reached a comfort level and operating rhythm that enabled us to move forward, we began to *reset* the business. At this stage of the process, we began to put plans in place to repair the damage. This is where we began making—or remaking—plans to recover and grow. As vaccination became common and people began to feel more comfortable venturing into brick-and-mortar businesses again, we restarted our event business and went back out to wine festivals. I also made the decision to pull our wines from wholesale distribution (a major reset!) to focus on more profitable retail sales at the winery and online. This reset effort continued well into the fall of 2022, when we had all the pieces in place to begin making plans to move into *offense* mode to recover lost revenue and market share that resulted from the pandemic.

As a result of leveraging this strategy, I positioned the winery to successfully recapture lost business and to chase new business opportunities in 2023 and beyond. The process took more than two years, but DSRO saved my business—and my sanity. Using this approach calmed me, slowed me down, helped me take things one step at a time, and kept my focus on what I could control.

You can apply this strategy to crises large and small. You may progress through these phases quickly or linger until you gain the focus you need to proceed, depending on the crisis at hand. Slow and steady wins the race.

LISTEN TO YOUR WHY

Once you have done the work to reinvent and realign to your why, enjoy the results! Feel your soul soar as you live your why. Always be the diva you were meant to be, and if you can't be a diva, be a firefighter! Remember, reinvention is a gift, not something to fear or avoid. Trust yourself, be kind to yourself, and believe in yourself. As you settle into your why-centered lifestyle, revel in the work you've done. Be proud of yourself for following your heart and deciding to prioritize feeding your soul. Wear your crown and celebrate your success and your courage. You're amazing! As you authentically live your why-centered lifestyle, your actions, impacts, and accomplishments will also inspire others far more than you may realize.

Our why changes as we grow and evolve as human beings. Isn't that great? To live a why-centered lifestyle, we need to continually stay in tune with our why. We need to pay attention and recognize when it shifts and we are no longer living a life that serves us. When that happens, we need to make the commitment to do something about it! We do ourselves, our loved ones, and the entire world a disservice by living life in a way that no longer actualizes our why.

If I have learned any lesson in my almost sixty years on this planet, it's that I never want to be in discord with what lights me up inside. We all have the power and can make the choice to live that life of light.

TIP 1 | *DON'T SKIP THE MAINTENANCE*

Think of a reinvention like a new car. When it's new, it feels great, runs great, and even smells great! To keep it humming along, you need to routinely change the oil, rotate the tires, and perform other maintenance on it. If you neglect that, the car may still run, but it becomes less efficient. If you forgo maintenance altogether, it will eventually break down. What was once clean oil lubricating the engine to keep you moving forward will become sludge in the bottom of your oil pan if not changed regularly. Your engine will require adjustments, and your tires will require air the more you drive around. Staying on top of this maintenance saves you time and headaches and prevents you from ending up stranded on the side of the road. Your why requires a similar kind of maintenance.

Check in with your why. Adjust it, repair it, or replace it as the demands of your life and your journey dictate. Schedule time for routine maintenance and reflection on your why on a regular basis. Refer to the *why* you clarified, defined, and documented in your reinvention plan. Does it still ring true? Has something changed?

TIP 2 | *REENGAGE WITH THE "REINVENTION FOR REBELS" PROCESS WHEN AND WHERE NEEDED*

Looking back, I realize I wasted precious years of my life living in discord with my why as my marriage died and as I toiled away in the corporate world. For a time, I was paralyzed by pain, doubt, and fear, and I was overly focused on *whats*. Hindsight is usually crystal clear, and this is certainly true in my case. Now that I see and understand that clearly, I strive to never do that again.

The process detailed in this book is a continuum. You can enter and exit it whenever and wherever you need to help you clarify, confirm, and commit to living your why. If you are feeling disconnection or discord with your why, go back and touch base with your core values and then spend time journaling with the prompts provided in chapter 3 for further clarification. You may already have the clarity you need, but if you're feeling stuck or afraid, revisit some of the Fight Fear with Facts tools and tips in chapter 4. Ready to commit to your reinvention path to your new or expanded why? Dip into the best practices in chapter 4 to help you make a plan. Use as much or as little of the process as needed to achieve the results you want. That's how it's designed. The more you do this, the better you'll get at it and the more natural it will feel.

It's my working theory—as evidenced by my experience navigating my most recent reinvention as author, speaker, and coach—that listening to my why on an ongoing basis is truly what makes this approach my lifestyle. Once I began to feel that shift and expansion of my why, I was able to take action to address it quickly because I was paying attention. Deciding to embark on the adventure to write this book could have resulted in a major upheaval in my life, but it didn't. Since I was already firmly aligned with my core values and had clarity about my calling to author this book, I entered my process for this reinvention by doing my homework to fight my fear and then developing and implementing a plan to make this book a reality.

Following my own advice and using this philosophy and process gave me the courage, motivation, and confidence to expand my why of making a connection and the freedom to incorporate this new element. This deliberate and focused realignment felt natural and seamless and directly increased my feeling of purpose and empowerment. I was also able to move quickly. I wrote this book in about six months after deciding to do it.

I now truly understand I have the power to live my best life on an ongoing basis. I also believe if I had ignored the shift in my why and the calling to follow the path to share my "Reinvention for Rebels" process with the world, I would've eventually reached a point where that decision would've impaired my personal growth and fulfillment. This calling was so strong that had I ignored it long enough, I believe I might have had to blow my life up again to retain that hard-won alignment and live this why. I've already learned that lesson the hard way. Instead, I navigated this reinvention by integrating these new elements of living my why into the framework of my life as an entrepreneur, which still brings me happiness and contentment. I felt like I was building a new room onto my house—a new sunroom that let even more light stream in.

REBEL QUEEN CHAPTER WRAP-UP

By living in relationship with and continually listening to my why and following its lead, I've discovered new opportunities to achieve balance, build commitment, and increase the positive impact I can make on my own life as well as the lives of others.

Don't be surprised if your why changes. And when it does, listen up! Life is short, and if you're feeling called in a new direction, why wait? I'm always keeping my heart open and thinking about my next reinvention, imagining the mirage of my next goal off in the distance. My next calling may be a little blurry and far away, but if I can see its outlines and move in that general direction as I live my best life, I know I'm positioning myself for remarkable things to come again and again.

Living a why-centered lifestyle means looking forward rather than looking down or backward. It requires staying the course even when crises arise and the going gets tough. It means loving and enjoying what we have but always keeping one eye open for what's next. As human beings, if we're not growing, we're dying. We can and should always keep our hearts open, listening to our why for clues about new and exciting opportunities that continually fill us with pride and purpose.

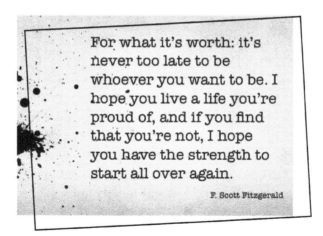

For what it's worth: it's never too late to be whoever you want to be. I hope you live a life you're proud of, and if you find that you're not, I hope you have the strength to start all over again.

F. Scott Fitzgerald

There is no passion to be found in settling for a life that is less than the one you are capable of living.

—Nelson Mandela

It's not the years in your life that count. It's the life in your years.

—Abraham Lincoln

You write your life story by the choices you make.

—Helen Mirren

Find out who you are and do it on purpose.

—Dolly Parton

You have brains in your head. You have feet in your shoes. You can steer yourself any direction you choose.

—Dr. Seuss

CHAPTER 6

6 | PRACTICING WHAT WE PREACH

...

This chapter is filled with stories about real people who are striving to live a why-centered lifestyle. I've changed their names to protect their privacy, but these are true stories of reinvention told by extraordinary people I've had the honor of working and walking with. By sharing these stories, as well as the examples and other revelations from my own reinventions in the preceding chapters, I want you to see the transformational power the concepts I preach—and practice—can offer you. I know I'll live this way for the rest of my life. Now that you know my secret, I hope you'll decide to do that as well.

These are stories of other rebel queens and a true rebel king. They shared their experiences, lessons, challenges, and outcomes with me as they used the concepts, tools, and tips in this book. I deliberately chose stories from people in different walks of life and in varied stages of growth and development to show how this philosophy can work for everyone, using the rebellious principles and approaches to their own ends and in their own time.

You're not alone in your quest. So many others are traveling beside you, cheering you on or looking to you for inspiration or support to commence their own journey of discovery. I hope these stories will inspire you as much as they inspired me.

THIRTYSOMETHING REBEL QUEEN
ADRENALYN FOR PRESIDENT

When COVID-19 hit, Roller Derby leagues shut down like everything else. There was no such thing as social distancing in a contact sport like Derby! AdrenaLyn trained hard to prepare for the 2020 season, and she was crushed when it all ended so abruptly after only one game as the world quarantined. Skating made her feel free, powerful, and safe. Not only was she a demon jammer on the track herself, but she was also sharing her knowledge and experience training rookie skaters. Derby made her feel seen and included as she found her why as well as her tribe.

When AdrenaLyn discovered Roller Derby, a bright light lit up inside her. She had never been particularly athletic growing up. Music was more her thing as she mixed it up in the marching band drumline in both high school and college on bass drum and snare. She had Barbie Rollerblades as a child, but when she strapped on those quad skates at her first Roller Derby tryout, she felt strength and exhilaration like never before. Skating with women of every age, background, shape, and size sparked something inside her. She always believed in inclusion and equity, but here it was in living color. She was hooked. She busted her ass to learn her craft and to train her body and mind not only to be the best skater possible but also to pay it forward and help others do the same.

When the initial quarantine lockdowns began to lift in summer 2020, people slowly began returning to outdoor activities. Indoor Roller Derby was still on hiatus, so she started an urban outdoor roller-skating group. As her "Roll Patrol" grew and thrived, her why of creating a free and inclusive community through skating revived as well.

In early 2022, Roller Derby leagues were starting to form again with immense uncertainty about health and safety. Her league had an opening for the role of president, a crucial leadership position to guide the resurrection of the sport. She felt called to step into this role because she knew she had the vision, expertise, and passion to bring the league back to life. Her success with Roll Patrol had also given her the confidence to expand into a more significant leadership role. She envisioned creating an environment of safety, clarity, and ease to bring skaters back to the track, but she was still intimidated about volunteering to be league president, especially in this turbulent time.

AdrenaLyn used one of my Fight Fear with Facts tools, creating a Fear Fable to tame and manage her fear and to discover the courage she needed. She pictured what would happen if she stepped up as president. She envisioned getting it right. She imagined using the leadership skills she had gained in other roles, including Girl Scout camp counselor and owner of a small pet-care business. She envisioned applying these skills in the familiar and safe environment of her Roller Derby space. She visualized balancing leadership, mentorship, and athleticism while affecting social change and bringing her Derby family back together. She reveled in the opportunity to create a special place where people could feel good about themselves because Derby is for everybody. She anticipated facing problems and solving them collaboratively with the rest of her leadership board, understanding that she already had skills and experience to do this job well.

Through this exercise of using a Fear Fable to imagine everything going right, she realized she was the most qualified candidate for president. She had the most time, knowledge, and resources for success in the role at this critical time. Her vision was so strong and affirming that she knew if she didn't step up, she would regret it. By visualizing what would go right, she overcame her fear and doubt of leading, and she took on the leadership challenge.

With that decision made, she got right to work. The league was still in crisis, having been essentially dormant for nearly two years due to COVID restrictions. To address this situation, she leveraged the DSRO crisis recovery techniques described in chapter 5. To bring the league forward from the defensive state caused by the pandemic lockdowns and social distancing measures, she first needed to stabilize then reset league operations. First, she reconstituted her board of directors, reinstated communications channels, and defined meeting rhythms. She contacted skaters to assess their interest in playing Roller Derby and surveyed their individual situations and concerns about returning to the rink. In partnership with her board, she skillfully created the strategy and plan to tackle the herculean task of resurrecting the league in this new and challenging environment, resetting rules for recruitment, training, and gameplay. Focusing on the pillars of safety, clarity, and ease, she and her board built a plan and a solid foundation for the future based on best practices, guidance, and lessons learned from authoritative sources. She manifested the inspiration and excitement needed to restart the league.

Six months later, the league was thriving under AdrenaLyn's leadership. Both veteran skaters and new rookies have returned to the track. They've all worked together to operationalize the desired environment she envisioned and implemented through her unique ability to lead in this difficult time. They had a few setbacks along the way as they worked to reset operations, such as skaters reporting COVID cases, but they continue to refine their operating procedures to safely gather and play Derby.

AdrenaLyn has even bigger ambitions as she listens closely to her why as it expands and grows. She's currently pursuing two parallel initiatives. The first is to start her own Roller Derby coaching and consulting business as many people have been asking her for private skating lessons and for help rebuilding other Roller Derby leagues. She's also working on plans to establish a nonprofit organization to serve as a worldwide Roller Derby collaboration and social network. She'll connect skaters, coaches, referees, and other Roller Derby devotees around the country and around the world to promote and celebrate the sport. She's starting by building a virtual gathering place and repository of information on all things Derby, with a dream of eventually creating a physical space to augment this virtual network. Her vision is to use this facility for practices, games, education, and as a social center focused exclusively on the Roller Derby universe.

She's listening to her why as it calls her to champion Roller Derby to a broader community in her neighborhood and around the globe. I'm so excited to see where this expanding why will lead her. Kick ass, AdrenaLyn!

FORTYSOMETHING REBEL QUEEN
JULIA TELLS FOOD TO F——K OFF

These are the reflections of fortysomething Julia Soul, who is currently at a crossroads of personal and professional reinvention as she expands the space in her life to live a why-centered lifestyle. She's already fought her fears and made a plan, but it'll still be a tough road ahead to stick with it and reach her reinvention goals. I asked Julia to work with my process to touch base with her core values and spend more time defining her why to give her clarity and inspiration for the difficult journey ahead.

Using the Know Your Core Values prompts in chapter 3 to explore and define her core values, Julia documented them as follows:

- Core value 1: Empower others by linking arms and walking with them.

- Core value 2: Love unconditionally and big, being the guidepost, the ear, and the nonjudgmental place of safety.

- Core value 3: Live my purpose again and again.

- Core value 4: Always show up with sincerity and vulnerability because the more open I am, the more open others will be.

Every day of Julia's childhood was filled with big love her mother gave her. She never built a real relationship with her father, who left and remarried when she was five. He was there but just by title. The constant was her mom, and she was a major force in Julia's life. They had a love story, but there were also times when it was a self-inflicted, haunting nightmare.

Her mom loved instant gratification, was extremely powerful, and believed in pushing through. Julia became a product of that environment. They shopped and spent money, went on vacations, and ate whatever they wanted. They stayed up late and had the best slumber parties! Julia's mom took care of her when she was hungover. She spent endless hours trying to figure out how to get Julia to "slow down" and stop drinking. Julia was convinced she could just have more whenever she wanted more. More food, men, alcohol, drugs—just more. By seventeen, Julia was in her first rehab. She married at twenty-one (out of spite from people telling her that she shouldn't), was divorced (and drunk) at twenty-five with two young daughters, and got sober at twenty-seven.

Julia powered through after the example her mom set. Power and perseverance, no matter what, became her why as she raised her girls as a single mom, took care of her mom for years before she passed from multiple sclerosis, and climbed the corporate ladder in banking and finance. Her why was like the Nike slogan: "Just Do It." Never show weakness, and don't let anyone know you need help. Julia doesn't have regrets or wish her past would've been any different. Getting sober and ruling the roost was everything she had to do to meet herself where she is now. She's ready for what's next. She's done the work to tame her lifestyle of extremes. She's taken the path of pain and hardship that leads to peace in these areas, and now she has one last area to surrender to and work through: food.

Julia loves food so much that she gained a hundred pounds over the last eight years. This weight now restricts her ability to move, travel, and fully enjoy the life she loves. She can't fully live the why-centered lifestyle that she's worked for with this impediment in her path. Julia's daughters are grown, and she's now married to the man of her dreams. She left the grind of the corporate world to start her own coaching and consulting practice. She's at peace and living a hard-won life of fulfillment except in one area: her weight. Julia wants a life of wellness and freedom.

Losing weight is a *what*, not a *why*, so I asked her to reflect on why she wants to shed the pounds. Using the Define Your Why journaling prompts in chapter 3, she discovered she wants to jet around the world with ease and physical strength. She wants to move her body in ways that are fulfilling and don't exhaust her. She wants to play with her grandkids someday. She wants to travel half the year in a camper with her beloved husband and three crazy dogs. She wants to create art. She wants to speak at conferences and share her story. She wants to serve a larger segment of women.

Julia has bravely fought her fear and made a plan to have weight loss surgery. She's ready, but this will be a challenging journey. Again, using the Define Your Why journaling prompts to gain increased clarity as she prepares to take this step, she further discovered she's yearning to be the woman she hasn't seen yet and walk this new path to see where it takes her. She wants to look in the mirror in six months and feel like she's shed something necessary to awaken new opportunities and possibilities her why is calling her to discover. She has a faith beyond her understanding. It guides her, and she trusts it. This exercise helped her define her *why* to share her experience that pain and hardship lead you to a peace like no other. She's embarking on this journey of enhanced physical and mental health and wellness to show the world it's okay to be broken, and by being broken, you can uncover your greatest gifts. Your liabilities truly are your best assets. She wants all the women to jump in the pool of grace with her and to feel through it, see it, be it, and discover that hindsight is a virtue.

Julia has an overwhelming calling to walk with women in business, life, growth, and pain. She's expanding her why and her mission to empower more women and to discover the freedom and beauty in it.

This reinvention isn't about the what of losing weight. Instead, it's about showing up for women by first showing up for herself with the gift of wellness of both body and spirit. This reinvention will allow her to escape boundaries and allow her to create time, space, and energy for new opportunities. It enables her to share her stories in new ways by eliminating the physical roadblocks standing in her way. She has the power to remove them. She's choosing herself so she can do more and be more for others in a healthy and empowering space.

FIFTYSOMETHING REBEL QUEEN
SYDNEY'S JOURNEY AFTER BOYS BECOME MEN

Sydney is a baseball mom. Wait. She *was* a baseball mom. Her two boys are now men and are departing the nest in rapid succession. Son 1 graduated from high school in 2020 (poor kid) and then entered the adult world of work. Son 2 graduated from high school in 2021 (poor kid) and headed to college. Before COVID, her life was jam-packed with baseball games, baseball trips, and baseball everything. She expertly balanced baseball-mom life with a demanding full-time job as a senior executive in the mortgage insurance industry. Life was chaotic and exhausting, but baseball was the family glue that held it all together for Sydney, her husband, and her boys. Unconditionally loving and supporting her family and cheering from her lawn chair behind the dugout was her why. It was the gift to herself and her family that fed her soul when corporate life ran her down.

Fast-forward three years and, aside from a league softball game her husband and son 1 play in, her life has become dominated by her demanding job. She has worked primarily from home since COVID hit, which provided some respite and relief with the added family time as well as the comfort of sweatpants and slippers instead of suits and heels. As she and her staff begin to return to the office in person and business travel resumes, she finds herself getting fully back on the corporate hamster wheel. This time, however, it is without the balancing relief of being a devoted and involved baseball mom to her boys, who are now beginning to live independently as the men she raised. She desperately needs a reboot—a major reinvention.

When I began working with Sydney, I recommended she start by using the tools in chapter 3, Know Your Core Values and Define Your Why. This is an important place to start, but it's not easy. It's been a long time since Sydney spent focused quality time on defining who she is, what she wants, and why. She truly wants to discover this, but she's also stubborn and tough and had trouble channeling the vulnerability required to honestly answer these questions and glean insights on her own. She also found it difficult to carve out the necessary time to deeply reflect on these topics. This will be an iterative process for Sydney, but the commitment to this ongoing work is what makes this process into a lifestyle. It's a lifestyle Sydney wants and will keep working toward.

The prompts provided in this book are helpful journaling tools for some to successfully use independently. Others like Sydney may benefit more from professional coaching or using a friend or mentor as a sounding board to bring these answers into focus.

To keep moving forward, Sydney and I began to talk through the exercises rather than having her independently journal her answers. By doing this, she was able to verbalize her thoughts, and together, we began to achieve some clarity, especially on her core values and her why. We'll continue to work together as she builds on this starting point to create the why-centered lifestyle she seeks.

Here's what we've discovered so far. When it comes to her work, Sydney does enjoy many of the challenges and opportunities she encounters working at a large firm despite the high stress levels. Connecting with people, solving problems, and achieving increased levels of personal and professional excellence all motivate her. Her work, however, doesn't provide her with the purpose she seeks. As we probed into what career fulfillment would look like, she revealed she longs for a seat at the table, an equal opportunity to participate in consistently impactful ways and be recognized accordingly. She doesn't want to be in an environment where her work can be deemed critical one day and redundant or obsolete the next. She wants to control the strategy and direction of her work. She's at the height of her earning potential and wants a demanding and exciting career opportunity where she can learn and grow. She wants to be treated as a true equal leader and partner in the success of her projects, her colleagues, and her company. She craves the security of knowing that her talents, capabilities, and contributions are seen and valued.

As her why begins to become clear, the next step will be to evaluate how her current situation meets her needs. She can then determine if her current work aligns with her why or if she should look for a different job or career and a company culture that would be a better fit. I believe imagining her ideal situation using the Flipping the Script tool in chapter 4 can help her identify the seat she wants at the right table.

Kids leaving the nest can be a tough and scary transition for many families and marriages. As Sydney and her husband navigate these challenges together, they find themselves resetting so many aspects of daily life and learning to communicate in new ways. They are reevaluating priorities and investments of time, money, and energy to determine how they best fit into their lives now. They are renegotiating new relationships with their boys, who are now men in the process of building their own independent lives. There are many moving parts here. As we talked about how she sees her life going forward, she envisions providing a beautiful and comfortable home for her and her husband, where she could entertain often and easily accommodate her sons and their families when they come home to visit—a welcoming respite to recharge and reconnect.

Another theme recently emerged from our ongoing discussions. Several years ago, Sydney started a nonprofit organization in her community to benefit local parks. She has a passion for philanthropy and for nature, so combining the two greatly appealed to her. COVID restrictions and her busy work life have put her nonprofit activities on the back burner. I suggested she reengage with it now to provide an outlet to explore an activity outside of work and family that sparks her soul and see where it leads her.

I'll continue to work with her as she navigates these crazy times and these difficult subjects. I'm very proud of her, and she has made an admirable start. Stick with it. The best is yet to come, Syd!

EIGHTYSOMETHING REBEL KING
BARNEY ALWAYS FOLLOWS HIS COMPASS

A dear friend and mentor of mine introduced me to Barney, and we scheduled a lunch at a local diner. Little did I know I was about to meet a reinvention rebel legend. A well-lived life does not even begin to scratch the surface of what I discovered over a meat loaf sandwich that day. We started with chitchat, but we quickly recognized a kindred spirit across that laminate-topped table.

Our stories of why-centered reinvention began to flow. As I listened to his amazing story and experiences, it cemented in my own mind the power of putting your why at the center of your life as a lifestyle choice and letting your core values serve as your foundational compass and guide. I want to be like Barney when I grow up.

Barney's why is living and sharing the power of love, belonging, and justice. In the three and a half hours we talked that day, he gave me a small window into his many and varied adventures of advocacy, love, compassion, and service. His life has had so many interesting and unexpected twists and turns. He went from homelessness as a teenager to pursue higher education and a career in health care and patient advocacy. He traveled extensively, focusing on helping those in underserved communities, including poverty-stricken border towns in Mexico and remote Native American reservations. He later led a large nonprofit organization. As he transitioned into "retirement," he has continued to find ways to love and serve others in ways large and small. Throughout his extraordinary life, he has formed deep connections with so many people in need through the power of unconditional love.

I've never met anyone so in tune with their core values. The alignment of Barney's core values and his why has become fully intertwined by continually following them throughout his life as his road map. We should all aspire to the level of alignment of our core values and our why that Barney manifests in his everyday life. This is not an easy feat to achieve, but the truth is that we all have the internal power to make that choice by listening to our why with an open heart. As I conclude this book, my love letter to all of you, I want to give you the gift of a lifetime of Barney's why-centered wisdom.

Barney's cornerstone core value is to stand up and fight for justice. This guides him as he uses every avenue at his disposal to address and correct injustice where he finds it. His why gives him strength to carry on, even if some might perceive his methods as completely unconventional or if he's not "allowed" to carry out his desired course of action. Barney absolutely and unassumingly embodies the concept that asking for forgiveness rather than permission can truly change lives. He sees what others don't see as he identifies uniquely impactful ways to seek justice in his community and the world. He leveraged this passion in the 1960s as he fought for civil rights shoulder-to-shoulder with African American friends in the Deep South. He also spent a lifetime advocating for young people aging out of the foster-care system, caring for them and using his voice and expertise to help their transition to independence when they had nowhere else to turn. With each unique experience to champion justice, he deepens and broadens his definition of this core value and why to inspire himself further. This is the true essence of living a why-centered lifestyle and a lesson I will never forget.

This next piece of wisdom Barney laid on me blew me away and will change my life forever. We are both driven people. I am a type A-plus fixer, and it is in both of our natures to try to fix something we see is broken. The difference is Barney knows the secret of "making room," focusing on the small thing you can do that makes a difference instead of trying to take on the world all at once. We need to respect our limits. "Making room" also means letting go of problems or challenges we can't control or fix. When we do this, we can save and redirect our own energy and talents for new ventures we never considered or even dreamed of.

It's never been easy for me to walk away from a challenge, even if I can't do anything about it. During the COVID-19 pandemic, however, I finally began to understand what an exercise in futility that approach was. I was being so unfair and unkind to myself, trying to fix things that were totally out of my control. I reached a breaking point during the COVID lockdowns, and in hindsight, what I did was discover the power of making room. By making different choices on how to invest my energy, I gained a sense of peace by cutting myself some slack and allowing others to tackle the issues I couldn't. I began to refocus on smaller pieces that I could influence and made room for others to take on other issues outside my control. By "making room," we also give others the gift of stepping in with new solutions and new energy. We can't take on new challenges if we don't first set down the ones we currently carry. I'm committed to implementing this philosophy in my daily life, doing all I can while being kind to myself and making room for opportunities and miracles.

Another core value Barney lives on every day is to respect and understand the impact of criticism. He makes it a point never to criticize before he takes a long look at himself first to see what he could have done better or differently before he responds in anger. Criticism can cut like a knife, but feedback and solutions that come from a place of caring, introspection, and authenticity can change lives.

Here's the most important core value and *why* that Barney lives every day. Everything you do must come from a place of love. He lives by the core value that everything belongs. It's simply a matter of figuring out how, where, when, and why it fits. There is no "other," and there is no "outside." This is his definition of unconditional love. Loving others as they are is second nature to him, and his lifetime of selfless acts has been inspired and fueled by love. He always looks at life through the prism of love. He believes if you act only out of love, you light a fire that will burn brightly in your life and in the lives of others. He also says if you want to do something but know you won't love yourself afterward, don't do it!

Barney thinks we've developed a self-imposed allergy to expressing unconditional love in our modern society. He thinks suffering is optional and usually self-inflicted. It invites and enables turmoil that can block or reject love. We all need to rediscover that love is an investment. When we give it freely and unselfishly without limits, the returns are remarkable.

Thank you, Barney, for sharing your love with the world and for giving me the gift of "making room" to share your story with others. You exemplify the power and majesty of living your life by the compass of your core values and your why, and you've truly inspired me to aspire to follow your trailblazing example.

FINAL THOUGHTS FROM THE REBEL QUEEN OF REINVENTION

I found incredible meaning and fulfillment in capturing the stories I've shared in this chapter that demonstrate the power of committing to a why-centered lifestyle.

I invite you now to create your own story of rebellion by taking the reins of your life guided by your core values and your *why*. Respect your fears, but fight through them with the knowledge you need and find the courage to live your best life. Make a plan and stick with it. And most importantly, develop a lifelong relationship with your why and listen to it intently. Give yourself, your loved ones, your community, and the entire world the gift of your light and legacy. Put on that crown, rebels, and wear it with pride. My why and I believe in you!

Mahatma Gandhi once said, "Be the change you want to see in the world." Let's change the world by accepting the challenge to rebelliously change the way we live our lives and spread the gospel about the joys of a why-centered lifestyle.

As Rebel Queen of Reinvention,
I practice what I preach.

—Destiny Burns

ABOUT THE AUTHOR

Destiny is a born and bred Cleveland girl. After graduating from high school, she enlisted in the US Navy as a Russian linguist to see the world. Twenty years later, she retired as a cryptologic officer and began a second career as a defense industry executive. She also served her community as a volunteer firefighter / EMT.

Upon turning fifty, newly divorced after a twenty-six-year marriage and with her only daughter fully launched into adulthood, she decided to leave the corporate world and move back home to Cleveland to open a "craft brewery-style" urban winery in a 1920s-era former auto repair garage. She is also an author, speaker, and coach, helping others live a why-centered lifestyle and wearing her crown as Rebel Queen of Reinvention with pride!

Printed in the USA
CPSIA information can be obtained
at www.ICGtesting.com
JSHW072147051023
49552JS00008B/15

9 798887 637853